THE
CHEQUERED
FLAG

THE
CHEQUERED
FLAG

By

DOUGLAS RUTHERFORD

COLLINS
ST JAMES'S PLACE, LONDON

First Impression,   May, 1956
Second   ,,   May, 1956

PRINTED IN GREAT BRITAIN
COLLINS CLEAR-TYPE PRESS: LONDON AND GLASGOW

To Meg

CONTENTS

ILLUSTRATIONS

9

ILLUSTRATIONS

MAPS

CHAPTER ONE

THE FIRST FIFTY YEARS

THE AIM of this book is to convey to those who do not have
the opportunity of witnessing them some idea of the character
of the great Continental motor races—their atmosphere and
background, the circuits on which they are run and the
people who take part in them.

It is hard to imagine the tremendous popular interest and
enthusiasm which these events arouse in Italy, France and
Germany, or the place which a great champion holds in the
people's minds. Each of the races has a character of its own,
due partly to the nature of the circuit, partly to the pro-
visions of the organisers, but most of all to the temper of the
crowds who come to watch. Perhaps the greatest difference
between English and Continental races is that most of the
latter are run on roads open to normal traffic for the rest
of the year. The knowledge that you have driven or will
drive your own car through those same bends adds the spice
of realism.

Only when chance brings you into close contact with the
men who race do you begin to understand the deep human
implications of the most perilous of modern sports. More
than driving skill is needed from a World Champion if he
is to race and win the day after his friend and pupil has been
unaccountably killed in practice. The crowds who come to
watch a Sunday's racing may have to wait a year before
they see their next Grand Prix. But four days later the

world's best drivers will already be practising on some other circuit, probably at the farthest end of Europe.

They seem normal enough, these men who ride the whirlwind. Whereas one may be calm and contemplative, with lazy speech and movements, another may seem as young and unsure of himself as a candidate for the Driving Test. They all have in common a certain quality hard to define. It is as if they were listening for a sound or watching for a light. When they take their place at the wheel of their car you realise they have found it.

Behind each driver are the unsung heroes, the racing mechanics. These are men who laugh at the idea of being paid for overtime, to whom sleep is an under-the-counter product which they take when they can. They'll strip a car to pieces and put it together again the night before the race, they'll stand by while it is driven at full speed for three hours in case it needs their attention, and when the finish comes with its bitter disappointment they'll load it on to its tender and take it to the other end of Europe to start all over again.

It is quite a circus, this little world that moves every week to some new centre. Drivers, racing managers, publicity men, mechanics, journalists and photographers; representatives from the firms supplying petrol, oil, tyres, brake linings and even the stuff you clean your windscreen with. It comes and goes between Wednesday and Monday and leaves behind it with the fading smell of racing oil, the blown newspapers, the black tyre streaks on tarmac roads, a curious sense of loss—and our day-to-day endeavours seem more trivial than before.

*   *   *

The construction of motors and the organisation of races is a matter of business. Driving a racing car is an art. The quality which most distinguishes the supreme performer from the mediocre one is an appreciation of line. There is an infinite number of lines which a car may take when rounding a particular curve, just as there are infinite possibilities for the outline of a Greek amphora or a piece of Venetian glass. Only the true artist can see the perfect line. The racing driver is different because he wields a new implement, placed in his hands by those foremost in the engineering achievements of this terrifying and exhilarating twentieth century.

Picture him as he sits in the single seat which has been constructed especially to his measurements. He wears the crash helmet required by regulations, goggles for his eyes and plugs to protect his ear-drums. Even in hot weather he must wear gloves to prevent his hands blistering; they are sprinkled inside with powder so that sweat shall not make them slippery. His shirt or jersey must fit neatly and tightly. His fireproof overall trousers are held by straps at the ankle and sometimes secured at the knee by sticky tape to prevent them ballooning in the wind. His footwear is a matter of personality and ranges from white suede shoes with high heels to hockey boots of soft leather. He sits, legs apart, with his feet in two separate wells; to the left the clutch pedal, to the right brake and accelerator, so adjusted that he can operate them both at the same time, one with his heel, the other with his toe. Depending on the car the gear lever may be beside his right or left thigh or between his legs. In the modern Grand Prix car the back of his seat tilts back a little and the steering-wheel is far enough forward to allow plenty of arm movement.

The instruments before him are few and simple—tachometer to show engine revolutions, oil pressure and water temperature gauges. The bonnet slopes away to give him an unhindered forward view. Two mirrors on either side of the tiny windshield enable him to see what is happening behind. He likes to be able to see both front wheels at the point where they meet the road, so that he can place his car to within an inch. The machine seems small with its wide-splayed, naked wheels, and gives no hint of the tremendous power imprisoned in it—until the engine is started.

From that moment on the driver lives in a world which is utterly beyond the conception of ordinary people. The great hurricanes which devastate the East American coast-line achieve a maximum velocity of 150 m.p.h. In a tempest of his own creation the racing driver lives through winds of almost 200 m.p.h. At the command of hand and foot he has several hundreds of horse-power, capable of punching his car from a standstill to 150 m.p.h. in 14 seconds, and brakes which will bring him from 180 to a crawl in 200 yards. To compete in a Grande Epreuve he must drive on the edge of disaster for three hours and more, negotiating corners at speeds which centrifugal force would make impossible if certain highly skilled techniques were not employed. On a fast, sinuous track like the Nurburgring he is faced with a corner every three seconds. On the city circuit of Monaco he must change gear every three seconds. At Buenos Aires he must go on racing under a tropical heat whilst even the spectators are being treated for sunstroke. At Spa a torrential downpour may flood the road so that spray from the car in front reduces visibility to that of a London fog. He must memorise every detail of the circuits over which he races, husband the machinery under his care and apply his race strategy in accordance with instructions of his team manager conveyed by signals from his pit. As opposed to the Stock Car racing driver who is paid to crash, his object is to keep the car on the road and to bring it to the finishing line in the best possible condition.

Of the qualities required to make a racing driver the first

is a sense of vocation—that inexplicable compulsion to race which draws a man day after day to the brink of doom. We all have our different ways of breaking the chains that bind our mortal feet to the earth, some petty and some noble. The real racing driver has the spirit that takes mountaineers to the summit of Everest and matadors to the bull-ring. But, like the test pilot whose life is at stake six miles above our every-day heads, he is the pathfinder for twentieth century man with his thirst to possess and exploit the creations of science.

Next come the inborn physical qualities; an especial sense of line and balance and a lightning quickness of reflex. He needs an instinctive ability to assess and adjust the forces under his control, engine power and braking power, against the forces which seek to destroy him, impetus and centrifugal force. It is often said that to be successful a driver must have brains—but he must have brains in the seat of his pants. The vital factor in gaining a split second on curves is wheel adhesion at the four points where rubber meets road surface. These four points must be his centre of consciousness and he must rightly interpret the messages that come to him through tyre, wheel, suspension, chassis and seat-cushion.

A man may be born with these qualities but to possess them is not enough. Experience must be added, so that the right man will build up a sound technique and, like a general who has studied the art of war in order to predict the moves of his foe, will react correctly to misbehaviour on the part of his own or someone else's car. Over and above all this he must have courage, for without courage who can face the unremitting danger, the frights, the disappointments and even the tragedies that racing inevitably brings?

That is why the great drivers in any decade can be numbered on your fingers, and that is why the death of such a man as Alberto Ascari means a serious loss to us all.

*　　　*　　　*

One must remember in connection with the history of motor racing that it is not absolute speed which counts most, but the speed which designer and driver achieve within the means at their disposal. For instance, the first Grand Prix of all, organised by the French Automobile Club in 1906, was won at an average speed of 63 m.p.h. The European Grand Prix of 1955 was won at 65 m.p.h. This does not mean that in half a century speeds have only increased by 2 m.p.h. The 1906 event was run over a fast circuit near Le Mans and the winning car's engine size was 13 litres. The 1955 race was run through the winding streets of Monte Carlo and the regulations in force limited engine size to 2½ litres. Since the earliest days the organisers of races and the Fédération Internationale de l'Automobile have framed their regulations so as to keep the speeds of Grand Prix cars within a reasonable limit. Their object has been not merely to provide a spectacle but to stimulate the development of road travel in all its aspects, from aerodynamics to road surfaces.

Motor racing has now passed its half century. It is easy to think of the racing machines of fifty years ago as antediluvian monsters. The picture arises of grim moustachioed figures in reversed caps gripping enormous steering-wheels as they race over roads where the ruts are six inches deep. Clouds of dust rise behind the leader and those following have to guess where the road is by the tops of the telegraph poles. Hand-brake and gear lever are outside the car and when tyres fail the mechanics slash the lacerated rubber from the fixed wheels with long knives. Yet in the uncompleted Paris-Madrid race of 1903 Gabriel in his Mors

Stirling Moss and the Mercedes Benz on their way to victory in the
British Grand Prix at Aintree   (*Photo Bernard Cahier*)

Mike Hawthorn and the winning Jaguar during the early stages of the
Le Mans 24 hour race   (*Photo Cahier*)

Juan Fangio driving the streamlined Mercedes Benz with which he won
the Italian Grand Prix   (*Photo Louis Klemantaski*)

Eugenio Castellotti at the wheel of the Lancia during the Belgian Grand
Prix   (*Photo Klemantaski*)

covered the 342 miles to Bordeaux at 65·3 m.p.h. The 18 litre De Dietrich racing car of 1906 achieved a maximum speed of 98 m.p.h. and by 1908 the Mercedes was already capable of over 100.

The earliest motor races were run from town to town—Paris to Rouen in 1894, Paris to Bordeaux in 1895, Paris to Vienna in 1902. Then in 1903 an attempt was made to stage a race from Paris to Madrid. In the early stages three drivers were killed and so many of the spectators lining the unguarded road had perished that the race was stopped at Bordeaux. During the following years all events were run on closed and properly policed circuits. The titanic struggles of the Gordon Bennet races from 1900 to 1905 were the very bedrock of motor sport. They were dominated by Panhard, Mercedes, Fiat and Richard-Brasier at speeds ranging from 31·8 to 54·5 m.p.h. The motor car, as a means of fast travel, was developing rapidly, and many manufacturers considered that the cost of engaging in racing was justified by its publicity value. By 1914 the overall speed of the French Grand Prix had been raised to 77 m.p.h. by the winning Delage.

After the First War racing did not revive for three years, but when it did its whole character was changed. The parting of the ways had come between purely Grand Prix machines and sports cars of a type which the public might conceivably buy. From now on the size and weight of Grand Prix cars was restricted according to a Formula decreed by the Fédération Internationale de l'Automobile, and altered in the light of advancing progress.

The '20s were the years of expansion and saw the inauguration of many varied races, among them three that still figure in the Sports Car Championship—the Le Mans 24-hour race, the Brescia Automobile Club's Mille Miglia and the Ulster Tourist Trophy. The years 1927 to 1930 were Britain's finest hour in Continental racing. For four consecutive years Bentley carried off the most coveted award in international sport—the Le Mans Grand Prix d'Endurance. But the warning note had struck in 1928 when the Italian Alfa-Romeo had begun their long string of successes in the Mille Miglia. In 1930 they came to Ulster in full force with a team of brilliant red cars and the finest trio of drivers in the world. A telegram from Mussolini just before the race ordered them to win. A few hours later they were able to signal: " We have obeyed." Nuvolari was first, Campari second and Varzi third. In 1931 they ousted Bentley from the dominant position at Le Mans and won the race for the next four years.

Benito Mussolini saw in this most contemporary of sports a means of bolstering Italian prestige and adding to the triumphs of Fascism. He decided that Italian cars should be supreme not only in Sports Car races but also in the Grand Prix field. The Alfa-Romeo which the obedient mechanics pushed out for the Italian Grand Prix in 1932 opened a new phase in racing. It carried an engine of 2·64 litres boosted by two superchargers and was capable of 140 m.p.h. In the hands of Nuvolari and Campari the new car won convincingly at 104 m.p.h. and so began the chain of successes which was to last four years. For although Alfa-Romeo ceased to participate officially, the cars were acquired by a certain Enzo Ferrari who continued to run them under the colours of the now famous Scuderia Ferrari.

In 1934 came Germany's reply to the Italian challenge. Hitler, himself a racing enthusiast, was not blind to the prestige value of success in this field. A prize of £40,000 was offered to the German manufacturer who put up the best show in 1934 Grands Prix. Naturally the well-established firm of Daimler-Benz went to work at once, but the comparatively new Auto-Union firm also decided to compete for the prize. Both companies were allowed to offset the cost of racing against armament contracts; between 1934 and 1939 they incurred a joint expenditure equal to £1 million.

The result was that Mercedes and Auto-Union produced the fastest and most exciting racing cars ever seen and further established the legend of German invincibility.

Only Alfa-Romeo and Maserati were able to meet the new challenge. They did so successfully in 1934 and 1935, but by 1935 the Germans had sharpened their teeth and were successful almost everywhere. The exception was a victory by Tazio Nuvolari driving an Alfa-Romeo in the very citadel of the foe, the Nurburgring; but this achievement was due less to the car than to the superlative artistry of the driver.

In these days when cries of protest are being raised at the speed of racing cars it is interesting to study the performance of the cars which won the major Grands Prix of the late thirties. To say that their capabilities were staggering is no exaggeration. Their 5·6 litre supercharged engines developed a brake horse-power of 646. Their maximum speed of 180 m.p.h. was not extraordinary. It was the acceleration which was phenomenal. From a standstill 60 m.p.h. was reached in 4 seconds and 140 in 11 seconds. As the car moved away from a slow corner the air was rent by the unearthly yell of the superchargers and the car seemed to the spectator to dissolve into the distance. The eye could scarcely credit it. In fact, only a handful of top-grade drivers were able to exploit the full possibilities of these projectiles. To the less skilful they were death traps and more than one driver of international repute came to grief in them. In the hands of Hermann Lang a Mercedes won the 1937 Tripoli Grand Prix at 134·25 m.p.h., and in the same year averaged 162·6 m.p.h., over 96 miles of the specially banked Avus track.

The extent of German domination is shown by the results of the 1939 Swiss Grand Prix, the last to be run before the outbreak of war:

1.	Lang	Mercedes
2.	Caracciola	Mercedes
3.	Von Brauchitsch	Mercedes
4.	Müller	Auto-Union
5.	Nuvolari	Auto-Union

At this point the Führer, perhaps fortified by the success of his venture on the race track, decided to assert the superiority of the Reich in other fields.

*   *   *

After the Second War the Fédération Internationale decided to leash the speeds of Grand Prix cars by a formula allowing engine sizes of 1½ litres supercharged or 4½ litres unsupercharged. In the period 1947–1951 it was once again Alfa-Romeo who came to the fore with cars known as the Type 158 and 159. Of the thirty-five races they entered they won all but four. As Laurence Pommeroy points out in " The Grand Prix Car," this was a record of success and reliability unparalleled in motor racing history. During 1949 the name Ferrari appeared in the entry lists, and even before the Alfa-Romeo concern decided to withdraw from Grand Prix racing the new cars were challenging them.

It is worth noting that up till this point records established in the 1930's were unbeaten. But now, after five years of mechanical development, cars of much smaller capacity were equalling the speeds of the pre-war giants of 600 h.p. The organisers of most of the big European Grands Prix decided to run their 1952 races on the basis of Formula two, which put the British Racing Motor out of the running before it had overcome its teething troubles.

During the 1952 and 1953 seasons the principal makes competing in Grands Prix were Connaught, Cooper and H.W.M., from Britain, Gordini from France, Maserati and Ferrari from Italy. Again one car was dominant, this time the four-cylinder machine designed by Lampredi, Chief Engineer of Ferrari. The results of the Grandes Epreuves held in these years are an almost unbroken catalogue of Ferrari success.

Then, at the very end of the 1953 season at Monza, came the Italian Grand Prix, when Fangio snatched victory for Maserati in the last seconds of the race.

For 1954 the F.I.A. introduced the new Formula One, stipulating a maximum of 750 c.c. supercharged or 2½ litres unsupercharged. Maserati's victory at Monza had renewed interest in Grands Prix, for the new formula did not necessitate any drastic difference in the design of the successful 2 litre cars. Lancia made no secret of the fact that they were building a car of completely new conception and had signed up Alberto Ascari to test and drive it. More than that, the international flavour was promised for the 1954 season for it was known that Daimler-Benz were preparing a Mercedes to enter the lists as soon as the new formula came into force.

In fact neither the new Lancias nor the German cars were considered ready to contest the first nine Formula One races of 1954. Ferrari and Maserati scored four wins each and Gordini one. The French Grand Prix was to be held on the fast Rheims circuit on July 4th and Mercedes had signified that they would be there. The team was managed by the same Alfred Neubauer who had engineered the successes of the late '30s. Their Number One driver was none other than the redoubtable Juan Manuel Fangio.

When the German machines were carefully rolled down the ramps of their transporter lorry for the first practice session it was evident to the spectators that a new era in racing had begun. Low and sleek, their chassis and wheels were completely enclosed in a streamlined body-shell. Beneath the silver skin were concealed revolutionary features of design—space-frame chassis, swing-axle rear suspension, fuel injection instead of carburettors and an engine that reclined on its side. In practice Fangio recorded a lap at 124·2 m.p.h. Soon after the race began the three Mercedes were in the lead. Hermann cracked up and retired but Fangio and Kling went on to take first and second places at 116 m.p.h., a pace so killing that the rest of the field was reduced to scrap.

This event sowed dismay in motor racing circles. There was much talk of the pre-war invincibility of Mercedes and some went so far as to predict that the dominance of the Stuttgart firm would kill Grand Prix racing. A fortnight later at Silverstone the new team was sadly discomfited and the dogged Fangio did well to drag a battered and tired *stromlinienwagen* into fourth place. Admittedly he went on to win the German, Swiss and Italian Grands Prix. But at Monza, Stirling Moss all but defeated the entire Mercedes team in his private Maserati and would have done so had his oil tank not split only ten laps before the finish. At Barcelona the Mercedes was never to the fore. In the early stages Ascari's new Lancia led the field and when he fell by the wayside Schell's Maserati took command. Finally it was Michael Hawthorn in the officially entered Ferrari who came through to a win which delighted the success-starved British enthusiasts even more than the Italians.

The Spanish Grand Prix was the last race and as the curtain came down the issue was still very open. Three Italian makes had shown themselves capable of tackling the Mercedes. The German cars were certainly formidable, but without the services of the racing genius Fangio, their first season might have yielded much less gratifying results.

Meanwhile, the sports car classics had been renewed and this form of motor racing was focusing even greater interest than before. Grand Prix racing with its specially built hybrid cars and its handful of crack drivers has a certain razor-edged, highly-tensed quality of its own. Here you undoubtedly see cars and drivers at their highest peak. But for the spectator there is especial interest in watching the performance of cars which he might possibly buy if he won the next football pool. It is to be regretted that the tendency in such races has been to allow manufacturers to run prototypes of a kind which no one ever sees on the road. However, what has been lost in practical interest has been gained in spectacle, for these so-called Sports Cars, unshackled as they are by Formula One, achieve higher speeds than the Grand Prix machines.

These contests, which exert a tremendous influence on the preferences of the buying public overseas, have a more international flavour; they attract not only Italian, French and in recent years German entries, but also a great number of British cars. A welcome feature of the post-war period has been the inclusion in the Sports Car Championship of the 12-hour race at Sebring, Florida, and the entry of American teams in the European races.

In this field the Italian Ferrari undoubtedly proved to be the most successful car of the decade, but at Le Mans Jaguars scored successes which brought to mind the great Bentley days. These victories warmed the hearts of all British followers of the sport and every year by plane, train, car and bicycle thousands of them made the pilgrimage to the one Continental circuit where they could hold their heads up.

So we came to 1955, a memorable, tragic and momentous

year in the history of motoring. Before it ended nearly a dozen drivers were to lose their lives, and over eighty spectators were to perish in the worst car crash in history. Yet at the same time the prestige of Britain's drivers was to rise higher than ever before. Five out of the six Sports Car Championship races were won by Britons, and a British driver was second in the Grand Prix World Championship.

The motor racing season had opened on the far side of the Atlantic. First round in the Formula One Championship was the Argentine Grand Prix. Immediately the scoring was thrown into confusion. With the temperature on the circuit rising to 140° Fahrenheit the race was run under truly infernal conditions. Practically all the drivers suffered from sun-stroke in varying degrees and were forced to seek refuge in the pits while others took their cars on. Only the two Argentines, Mieres and Fangio, were able to drive their cars single-handed throughout the race. Even Fangio was forced to stop repeatedly to sluice himself with cold water. Whilst he continued to drive at breakneck speed through the furnace his wife and mother knelt in his pit and prayed for his safety.

The official results show how frequently each car changed hands:

1.	Fangio	Mercedes
2.	Gonzalez/Trintignant/Gonzalez/Farina	Ferrari
3.	Farina/Maglioli/Trintignant/Maglioli	Ferrari
4.	Hermann/Kling/Moss	Mercedes
5.	Mieres	Maserati
6.	Schell/Behra	Maserati
7.	Musso/Schell	Maserati

Although they figured on the Sports Car Championship calendar neither the 1,000 kilometre race at Buenos Aires nor the 12-hour race at Sebring attracted important factory

THE INTERNATIONAL CALENDAR
FOR 1955

World Championship Formula 1 Cars

Jan.	16.	Buenos Aires	..	..	Argentine Grand Prix		
May	22.	Monte Carlo	..	..	Monaco	„ „	*
June	5.	Spa—Francorchamps		..	Belgian	„ .,	*
July	3.	Rheims	..	.. ..	French	„ „	†
July	16.	Aintree	..	.. ..	British	„ „	*
July	31.	Nurburgring ..		.. ..	German	„ „	†
Aug.	21.	Berne ..	..	.. ..	Swiss	„ „	†
Sept.	11.	Monza	..	.. ..	Italian	„ „	*
Oct.	23.	Barcelona	..	.. ..	Spanish	„ „	†

Drivers to be allotted   ..   ..   .. 8 points for first place
6 points for second place
4 points for third place

The driver who records the fastest lap wins 1 point.

World Championship for Sports Cars

Jan.	23.	Buenos Aires	..	..	1,000 kms. race	
March	13.	Sebring, Florida	..	..	12-hour race	
April	30		..	..	Mille Miglia	*
to May	1.	Italy				
June	11/12.	Sarthe	..	..	Le Mans, 24-hour race	*
Aug.	28.	Nurburgring ..		..	1,000 kms. race	†
Sept.	17.	Dundrod, Ulster	..	..	Tourist Trophy	
Oct.	16.	Sicily	..	..	Targa Florio	
Nov.		Mexico	..	..	Carrera Panamericana	†

Races marked * are described in this book.
Races marked † were cancelled after Le Mans.

entries. The first was won by the local pair Valiente and Ibanez in their Ferrari. In the second a field of nearly 20 cars set off on the endurance test. The American driver Phil Walters and the British driver Mike Hawthorn took turns at the wheel of the Jaguar entered by Briggs Cunningham of the U.S. and brought it into first place.

So when the centre of interest shifted across the Atlantic to Europe honours were even between the Italian and British cars. The next event was the Mille Miglia. Jaguars had not entered for this race. Mercedes-Benz most definitely had.

CHAPTER TWO

THE DRIVE OF THE CENTURY

Mille Miglia. Brescia. 30 April—1 May

THREE DAYS before the Mille Miglia began, the city of
Brescia was in the grip of race fever. Even the swallows,
returning with the spring from southern climes, forgot to
build their nests and careered in hysterically screaming
bunches over the roof-tops. Messenger boys on bicycles had
a wild look in their eyes as they swerved past pedestrians,
their lips rounded to reproduce the sound of a racing
exhaust pipe. Piazza Vittoria, Brescia's modern central
square, was black with people. On both the east and west
sides a rectangular space had been partitioned off by wooden
palisades. Young men, boys and girls crowded the barriers,
staring with hungry, speculative eyes at the empty patches
of roadway where competing cars would be inspected.
Inside, seated at tables laden with documents and shaded
by broad red and white umbrellas, sat official-looking men.
They too were waiting. Above their heads a dozen placards
announced the nature of their business. " Mille Miglia.
Coppa Franco Mazzotti. Categoria Sport."

The normal architectural façade of the Piazza, pride of
Italy's modern town-planners, was almost completely
obliterated by banners advertising every conceivable brand
of petrol, oil, sparking plugs or tyres. Special police inter-
preters moved among the crowd, their armbands saying

27

español, deutsch, français or *english*. In front of the cafés lining the square all the tables on the pavement were filled.

Suddenly the thick murmur of the crowd checked. Overhead the swallows were screaming again. A new sound, unmistakable to the expert ear, had cut through the din of everyday traffic and all heads turned. Into the square, like a fighting bull into a crowded arena, shot an angry red car. Making furious play with his accelerator pedal, the goggled driver forced the nose of his car through the human wall. But, low seated as he was, he could not tell which was north, south, east or west. The instant he stopped to regain his bearings he was submerged under a dozen autograph-hunting small boys. Two *carabinieri* forced their way to his side and directed him to the sanctuary of the enclosed rectangle. A few minutes later the announcer on the public address system sent his voice booming out over the square.

" The magnificent sports car now in the scrutineering enclosure is the Maserati of Carpano, competitor in the 2,000 c.c. class."

When the number which it would carry in the race had been painted on its bonnet and side, the Maserati was rolled in front of the tables where officials of the Automobile Club of Brescia waited to inspect it and ensure that it was a genuine example of a car in series production. The seals were placed on vital sections of the machinery—an insurance that no replacements could be made before or during the race—and then the driver again took his seat in the car. This time he made no mistake. The crowd which had pressed forward at the sound of the starting engine leapt for its life as the Maserati came snarling out of the enclosure. The red car accelerated away as if the Mille Miglia were beginning at that very moment. The autograph hunters had to be content with the tang of racing oil hanging in the sunny air and the harsh echo of the car's engine as it departed homicidally along the Via Dante.

And there were still three days to go.

As far back as 11th September, 1899, a motor race had been organised on the Brescia–Cremona–Mantua circuit, but the first Mille Miglia did not take place till 1927. Even then the conception was revolutionary—to run a race over a thousand miles of open roads, linking Brescia with the capital. It was the brain-child of four members of the Automobile Club of Brescia. Franco Mazzotti, much missed by lovers of the Mille Miglia, is dead, though his name is connected permanently with the race. Count Aymo Maggi, Renzo Castagneto and Giovanni Canestrini still lend the colour of their personalities to each succeeding race. Aymo Maggi was himself a racing driver of note in the '20s and scored a number of successes with Bugattis. He competed in the first Mille Miglia and finished the course on the huge 8 litre Isotta-Fraschini, the only car in its class, at a speed only a little below the winner's. He and the Contessa Camilla are known to all British competitors, for their unbounded hospitality makes the Mille Miglia an almost family affair. The big house at Calino, with its liveried, white-gloved servants, its unmatched food and wine, is an oasis in the relentless round which is the racing driver's lot.

Giovanni Canestrini is the technical expert; his face is now known to millions of television watchers, who will remember his amazingly shrewd assessment of the prospects for the 1955 race.

Castagneto, the *éminence grise* of the race, works shuttered away in his office within an office within an office. Upon him rests the main burden of organisation. Rather a terrifying figure, he reserves the favour of his startlingly youthful smile for the men to whom he waves the chequered flag.

29

He has done so now for twenty-two Mille Miglias; except for the freak war year 1940 when the race was run on a closed circuit, its character has remained unchanged. Starting from Brescia, it has taken competitors to Rome down one side of Italy and back up the other. The course has been altered 14 times but nearly always the distance was around 1,600 kilometres, 1,000 miles. In distance covered that is the equivalent of Aberdeen to London and back, but to reproduce the equivalent you would have to place the Scottish Highlands athwart your route.

Needless to say, such a project was met with official scepticism. However, a person whose voice carried authority in the Government saw the possibilities of the event and gave it his blessing. Even Mussolini, himself an enthusiast for speed, sent his congratulations to the winners of the first race. Those first Mille Miglia cars were of a type now only to be seen at rallies of the Vintage and Sports Car Club— proud, high bonnets, strutted mudguards, rigid suspension and superchargers. Drivers still favoured reversed caps rather than helmets, punctures were frequent and a saloon sports car was unheard of. Most of the roads were rough and stony. The cars left long clouds of dust behind them and passing was a hazardous undertaking. To finish at its average speed of 48 m.p.h., the winning O.M.—a car manufactured in Brescia itself—was on the move all one day and all one night. It had traversed thirty provinces of Italy, passed through twenty important towns and countless villages whose pavements were crowded with wildly enthusiastic spectators. What is more, the roads, though carefully supervised, had not been closed to ordinary traffic.

The event had been a success and from now on Brescia's Mille Miglia was established on the international calendar. It has remained the classic road race ever since, unparalleled

30

by any other event in the world. Essentially Italian in character, it has been almost exclusively the preserve of Italian cars and drivers. Until the historic race of 1955 only one foreign driver had ever been victorious. No British driver had finished in the first four. No more than five makes of car had ever won and of these O.M., Mercedes and Lancia had only done so once. Two makes had dominated the event. From 1928 to 1938 Alfa-Romeo's chain of success had only been broken by Caracciola's Mercedes in 1931. More than that, in the period 1932–1938 only a couple of Delahayes prevented them from filling the first four places every year. After the war it was, to a lesser degree, the turn of Ferrari. This firm won the race every year from 1948–1953. British successes in twenty-one races were confined to half a dozen wins in one or other of the minor classes, notably those of George Eyston in an M.G., in 1933, and of Tommy Wisdom on an Aston-Martin in 1951 and '52. These were sporting and notable achievements in themselves but a mere drop in the ocean of the Mille Miglia.

There is a whole history to be written about the Mille Miglia but even the winner of a Fellowship in Analytical Research would falter in the face of such a task. How can one set out to describe a race in which hundreds of drivers start off at minute intervals and are lost in the depths of the Italian countryside for anything from ten to twenty hours? Only the drivers themselves know what really happened and they won't tell. Journalists who ride in the passenger's seat have recorded their impressions in stirring terms, but they can only relate the story of one car—and until 1955 that car was never the winner.

Nevertheless, certain great figures and achievements rise up out of the mists of past Mille Miglia. Biondetti won the race in 1938 and again in 1947, '48 and '49. At the end of

31

the last Mille Miglia before his death his car broke down at the very gates of Brescia, but he pushed the heavy saloon all the way to cross the line as a finisher. Pintacuda leapt from obscurity to fame when he defeated all the crack drivers in 1935 and repeated the exploit in 1937. Nuvolari, that greatest of all drivers, whose way with a racing car had some quality that brought a lump into the throat and whose presence on the scene was akin to that of Casals on the concert platform or of Manolete in the bull ring, was the winner in 1930 and 1933 and came second in 1934 and 1937. Yet his failures were more remarkable than his successes, none more so than his last race in 1948. Driving a Cisitalia of only 1,100 c.c. he was the fastest man to Rome. When the bonnet cover failed to go back into position after his refuelling stop in the capital he tore it off and began his assault on the mountain section with a bare engine. By the time he reached Reggio Emilio, he had lost a mudguard his shock absorbers were useless and he had no brakes. Still in the lead he was champing to whip the car on but the owner of the Cisitalia forced him to retire in the interest of his own safety.

Now Tazio Nuvolari, the Flying Mantuan, is dead; but every driver who finishes the Mille Miglia salutes his memory as he passes through Mantua. For the last two years the circuit has been altered to include his native city and a special award, the Gran Premio Nuvolari, goes to the driver who records the best speed over the triangle Cremona –Mantua–Brescia.

Whenever prospects for the Mille Miglia are being discussed, certain great races of the past are remembered. First, the duels between Nuvolari and Varzi. In a race when the competitors are started at minute intervals and the winner is he who covers the course in the best time, it is considered a great advantage to start after your rival. In

32

Mille Miglia. The Triumphs of Margairez, Scott-Russell and Steed
lined up for their dawn start in Brescia. The number painted on each car
indicates its time of departure   (*Photo Rotofoto*)

Mille Miglia. Moss and his Mercedes squeeze at racing speed between two walls of human beings. Moss's eyes assess the corner which he is about to take while his navigator Jenkinson is already consulting his notes to see what lies beyond   (*Photo Publifoto*)

Mille Miglia. The historic moment. At 5.35 on Sunday, 1st May, Moss enters the Viale Rebuffone to take the chequered flag   (*Photo Rotofoto*)

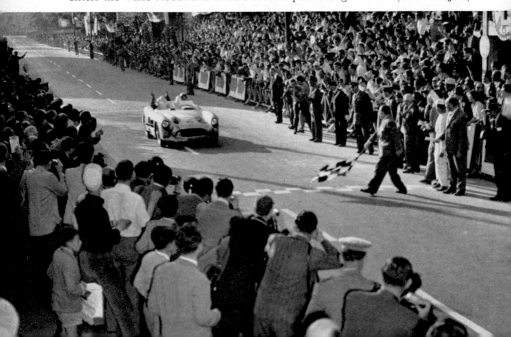

1930 Nuvolari started ten minutes later than Varzi. After 970 miles he caught him up at Desenzano and the howl of Nuvolari's supercharger behind him told Varzi that the race was lost. They fought it out wheel to wheel over the final kilometres, but it was a duel in the interest of honour. Nuvolari was already ten minutes ahead. Then, in 1934, the tables were turned. Varzi started after Nuvolari and caught him up between Ancona and Venice.

It was Bracco, driving his saloon Ferrari in 1952, who smashed the legend that to win you must start behind your rival. That was the year Mercedes made a determined effort to take the Mille Miglia, and at Florence Kling was in the lead. The defence of Italy rested on the young Bracco, four minutes behind him. Ahead were the Appenines, the treacherous Raticosa and Futa Passes. Bracco had won the sobriquet of King of the Mountains. Now he proceeded to justify it. When both the drivers had gone past the Bologna control the stop watches showed that Bracco had wrested the lead from Kling and gained over five minutes on the rain-soaked mountains. But Bracco, already tearing along the dead straight section to Piacenza, did not know that he was in the lead by 1 minute and 10 seconds. With Kling behind him on the road he had to drive all out to Brescia, and before he knew that he had won he had to wait on the finishing line for the vital minutes to tick away.

Facts such as these were bread and butter to the citizens of Brescia. Long before the Mille Miglia, in cafés and on street corners, you could hear the famous names being bandied to and fro with a wealth of gesture and expression which re-created the event before your very eyes. The Bresciani call the week before the Mille Miglia their *settimana di passione*. Up and down the length of Italy, appetites had been whetted by the spectacle of fast cars passing as drivers attempted to familiarise themselves with the thousand-mile circuit. But Brescia, the very cradle of the race as well as the start and finish, was subjected to an intensified form of preparation. In the city and surrounding villages garages had been turned into racing stables. Mercedes were in the big Fiat garage, the French contingent out at Pilzone on the Lake of Iseo. Any moment as you rounded a corner in your car you might be confronted with the spectacle of a race car coming towards you at over a hundred miles an hour.

The real feast was to be enjoyed in Piazza Vittoria, though, as the cars presented themselves for scrutiny. Many of the private entrants had gone through the formalities on the Thursday, but Friday was a day of true fulfilment. The Aston-Martins appeared early amid a welter of Porsches, D.B.s, Fiats and Maseratis. The east side of the square was still cool and shaded by the high buildings. Then at about eleven and in an awed silence, a jeep drew a long trailer into the enclosure. On it were two smooth, silver projectiles, beautifully finished and with the suggestion of speed in every square millimetre of their streamlined bodies. The Mercedes of Fangio and Kling. The drivers themselves had appeared in the enclosure as if by magic and the loudspeakers called for a salute to *Juan Manuel Fangio, il campione del mondo*. The team of photographers postured and squatted to angle their pictures and the crowd applauded. The quiet man in the grey suit and floppy cap smiled his lazy smile and gently raised a hand in acknowledgment.

As the first Mercedes trailer pulled away the second one arrived. These were the cars of Hermann and Stirling Moss, different from the others in that they had open cockpits with accommodation for a passenger and a double cowling behind the head-rests. The Mercedes mechanics had already painted on Moss's car the correct number 722, an indication of the precise minute at which he would start

34

his race on Sunday morning. On the silver paint of the cowling behind the driver's seat a Union Jack stood out crisply.

All Friday the crowd waited in vain for their idols, the Ferrari team. Not till Saturday morning did they show up. Then they drove into Brescia at racing speed, nose to tail, the man in the front car waving the oncoming traffic to the side of the road. To a modern Italian the note of a Ferrari is as unmistakable as the sound of distant bag-pipes to a Scotsman.

" Le Ferrari! Le Ferrari! "

Hardly had the cry gone up than the tight bunch of cars was in the square, as wicked and dangerous as a flight of hornets. The crowd converged in passion and then, like the Red Sea before the Children of Israel, divided. The Ferraris passed into the scrutineering enclosure.

When they had gone, everyone breathed a deep breath. In twos and threes the crowd drifted away to lunch. This afternoon *la siesta* was important. There would be precious little sleep in Brescia on Saturday night.

As the last hours before the 1955 race passed swiftly on their way it began to seem that certain traditions of the Mille Miglia were going to be broken. To begin with, the weather was set fair and there was every chance that for once the conditions would be ideal. The entry was as cosmopolitan as ever. The French were strongly represented in the smaller classes and in the big car class there were Aston-Martins and Austin-Healeys from Britain and the Maseratis and Ferraris of Italy. But the imponderable factor was undoubtedly the challenge from the Daimler-Benz factory at Stuttgart.

Mercedes were this year making their most determined effort to take the Mille Miglia since Caracciola, on a giant white 7 litre car with screaming supercharger, had dis-

35

comfited the Alfa-Romeos, twenty-four years earlier. Apart
from the five closed cars entered in the Gran Turismo
category, they were running 300 S L R sports cars in the
over 2,000 c.c. class. They were known to have a dozen
machines to choose from. They had brought a team of
sixty technicians to Italy, headed by the redoubtable
Neubauer—a man of such weighty presence that his passage
literally made the floor tremble. Karl Kling alone had
expended over £1,000 worth of petrol in practice. No detail
had been overlooked in their preparations. The 300 S L R
is normally fitted with a two-spoke steering-wheel. When
Stirling Moss tried his car he asked if he could have one
with three spokes. He likes to drive with his arms at full
stretch and his thumbs hooked round the spokes at 10 and
2 o'clock on the dial. The new steering-wheel was designed,
constructed and fitted to the car within three days.

Their drivers were a formidable array. Fangio had
already driven the Mercedes Formula One car to victory in
six Grands Prix in 1954 and '55. Kling had been second in
1952 and in 1953 he had led the race before crashing near
Siena. He deserved to win as much as anyone in the entry
list. They were supported by two youthful drivers, both
capable of great things—Hans Hermann and Stirling
Moss.

Stirling Moss is the only Englishman to whom the term
" professional racing driver " fully applies. Now that he has
reached the age of twenty-six his life is entirely dedicated to
this one end.

His father had dabbled in motor racing so the boy was
born with a shot of mercury in his blood. Riding had been
his early passion and astride a horse at his home on the
farm at Tring or at his school, Haileybury, he had acquired
the quickness of reflex and sense of balance so essential to
a good driver. Even before he was old enough to qualify

for a driving licence he was careering round the family estate on his sixteenth birthday present, a three-wheeler Morgan. As soon as he had his licence he invested his savings in a Cooper. His talent was immediately apparent. By 1948 many events were being organised for the small and inexpensive 500 c.c. racing cars. This was the school in which Moss learnt his technique, winning twelve of the fifteen races he entered that year. He showed that he had exceptional gifts and was soon offered the wheel of bigger cars, notably the H.W.M. Grand Prix car and the Jaguar sports.

During the years 1951–1954 he won the Gold Star of the British Racing Drivers' Club four times and climbed rapidly to fame. His mounts ranged from Jaguar in the sports car field to Cooper-Alta in Grands Prix. Highly successful in British meetings he failed to score any real successes in Continental races. But his motoring activities were extensive. He was second in the Monte Carlo Rally and competed three times running in the Alpine Rally without losing a single mark.

Until 1954 he stuck to British cars but in that year his father purchased him a Formula One Maserati. With this car he proved that he was among the best drivers, but consistent bad luck again kept him from winning any of the Grandes Epreuves. He was firmly in second place in the British Grand Prix when eliminated by engine failure. In the Italian Grand Prix he had won a commanding lead from the pick of the official Continental teams only to be put out at the last minute by yet another mechanical failure. The only place where luck seemed to favour him was the new Aintree circuit.

During the following winter he signed up to drive Mercedes-Benz sports and racing cars for the 1955 season.

Moss's entire activity throughout the year revolves around

cars and racing. His work takes him from one end of Europe to the other and often across the Atlantic. When he is not racing he is busy with the other side of the business —purchasing pieces for the Maserati he still owns and runs, dealing with advertisement contracts, press interviews, requests to open charity bazaars and a hundred other matters.

Though he still regards Tring as his home he now has his own London flat in Challoner Street. He absorbs vast quantities of Coca-Cola but never drinks alcohol, although he has a decided preference for food cooked with wine. Only recently he has begun to smoke. He considers that in order to race he must keep himself in good condition. He makes it a rule to go to bed by ten the evening before a race. He sleeps late and eats neither breakfast nor lunch before going out to the course where he is to race. He is always there in good time, discussing points with his mechanic or team manager, putting on his racing clothes—soft leather boots, overalls held at ankle and wrist, broad waist-belt to support stomach and back muscles. He is very quiet and uncommunicative before a race, building up his concentration for the job ahead and saving his energy.

On the ground he is a stocky, rather curt and uneasy person. Once in a car he is transformed.

His driving style is very individual and based on the principle that to last a three-hour race or more you must be relaxed. He sits well back, arms and legs at full stretch. He is recognisable from far away by the particular set of his head. He never looks as if he is hurrying and is above all a courteous driver. He is a master of the four-wheel drift and his facial expression hardly changes as he straightens his car out of a hundred mile an hour slide.

Moss himself is one of Fangio's warmest admirers and never hesitates to say that the Argentine is the first driver

38

in the world. But should Fangio ever decide to give up racing Moss has all the qualities required to step into his shoes as World Champion.

Now that we have the man this is surely the moment for Britain to produce the car. In the meantime Moss's victories must be chalked up to the credit of Germany.

When one considered the history of the Mille Miglia the chances of a British driver winning seemed so remote as to be hardly worth considering. It was not generally known that Stirling Moss had toured round the circuit during practice and amid the hazards of ordinary Italian traffic had averaged 75 m.p.h. It was his fifth Mille Miglia. Up till now he had always been at the wheel of a British car but had never reached the finish. This time he had put in a lot of practice, starting over a month before. During the days preceding the Mille Miglia he gave everyone the impression that his real self was far away, that in his mind's eye he was at the wheel of his car somewhere out there on the thousand mile circuit.

As Lancia, winners the year before, were not competing, the responsibility for carrying the Italian colours rested with Ferrari. Of their four pilots Umberto Maglioli had already scored a resounding victory in the Mexican Carrera Panamericana and Piero Taruffi was in the ace position of being last to start. A skilful and experienced driver with a record going back to pre-war races, he was perhaps the only man who might claim to have memorised the entire circuit. In 1952 and '53 he had been up with the leaders at various stages and in 1954 he had led at well over half distance. In all three years he had been forced to retire. In 1955 he was the favourite.

Over six hundred vehicles were entered for the 1955 race. They ranged from the tiny Isettas, which can best be pictured as a four-wheeled version of the Bond Minicar,

39

to the 4·4 litre six cylinder Ferrari. Divided into eleven classes they would start at half-minute intervals from 9.0 till 10.00 p.m. on Saturday evening, and then all through the night at one-minute intervals till 7.28 on Sunday morning. At 7.30 when the last car was on its way, High Mass would be celebrated in Brescia Cathedral.

As midnight approached, the scene at the start was a fantasy. Grandstands had been built on either side of the Viale Rebuffone. In the centre of the roadway a bright yellow wooden ramp had been erected. A battery of floodlights was trained on it. Behind stretched the queue of waiting cars, their crews strapping on helmets, saying tender farewells, swilling final drinks and biting their nails in mounting degrees of nervous tension. These were not hard-bitten professionals on hybrid sports cars but amateurs whose great adventure in the year is the Mille Miglia. Their mounts were mostly Fiat saloons, perfectly standard except for special tuning of the engine and a marked absence of silencer.

As each crew's turn came they drove on to the flat top of the ramp, in full view of everybody. For thirty seconds they sat under the blaze of the lights while the photographers' magnesium bulbs flashed and the television cameras peered down. Now and then a special cheer went up as the Bresciani recognised a driver from the home town. Then the flag would fall, the tyres would squeak and the car would career down the ramp. This quick start, though murder for the shock absorbers, was as important for prestige as hitting your drive off the first tee at St. Andrews. In a few seconds you would be out of the tunnel of light with the roads of half Italy ahead of you. Even before your tail light had disappeared round the first bend another car would be up there glittering on the ramp and you would be forgotten. It was the moment of deceit. The moment of truth would come you knew not when, round any one of five hundred iniquitous curves.

Just about midnight the atmosphere changed. The first of the true-blue sports cars had been creeping up the queue towards the ramp. Behind it was a purposeful line of Panhards, D.B.s, Stanguellinis. After the staid, repetitive Fiat saloons they were a welcome promise of the drama to come.

And so, all night it went on, a car a minute, while the drivers of the biggest machines slept the sleep of normal men.

Just after 2.0 the first car of the Gran Turismo class was started. It was a private car in everyday use and was driven by Ferrante Viola, the miller from Lonato, ten miles down the road. He travelled alone because he could not persuade anyone to risk their neck with him. At 4.17 the American driver, John Fitch, took away one of the saloon Mercedes. He was followed a minute later by Paul Frere on the first Aston-Martin with the photographer Louis Klementaski as passenger. The sun was already up when the Triumphs and Maserati's got going. It was high enough to shine in the eyes of the Mercedes and Ferrari drivers as they started on the wild dash to Verona, forty-two miles out.

At 7.22, when Moss took his Mercedes cautiously down the ramp, there were only half a dozen more cars to come. Beside him in the passenger's seat he had Denis Jenkinson. *Barba rossa,* as the Italians called the bearded journalist, had eighteen feet of paper on rollers—Moss's notes on the route based on five years' experience. Engine and wind noise made it impossible to talk in the cockpit but they had evolved signals by which Jenkinson could indicate ' left,' ' right ' and ' flat out.'

When Taruffi, the backmarker, had shot out of town at 7.28 a.m. with the devil on his heels, there was nothing for Brescia to do except possess its soul in patience and wait for

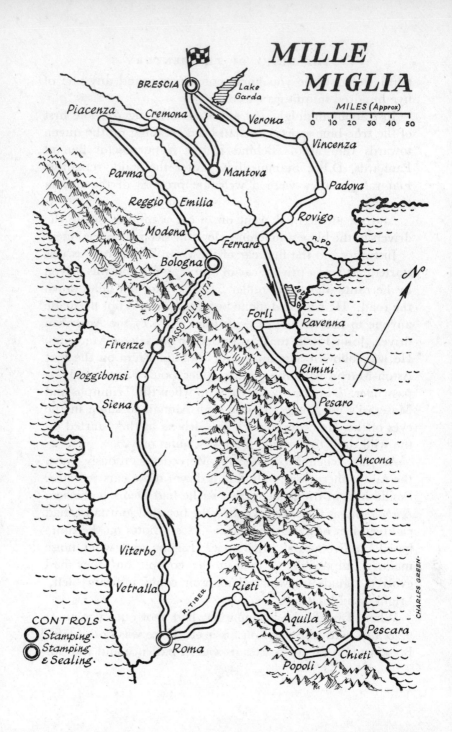

MILLE
MIGLIA

BRESCIA
Lake Garda
Piacenza
Cremona
Verona
Vincenza

MILES (Approx)
0   10   20   30   40   50

Parma
Mantova
Padova

Reggio   Emilia
Rovigo

Modena
Ferrara
R. PO

Bologna

N

PASSO DELLA FUTA

Forli
Ravenna
R. PO

Firenze
Rimini

Poggibonsi

Siena
Pesaro

Ancona

Viterbo

Vetralla
Rieti

R. TIBER

CONTROLS
○ Stamping.
◎ Stamping
   e Sealing.

Roma

Aquila
Pescara

Popoli
Chieti

CHARLES GREEN.

news to trickle through from points around the course. All in good time the surviving competitors would return to the Viale Rebuffone. The leader of the smaller cars was already well on his way back from Rome and might reach Brescia soon after midday. But the minds of everyone were on the big cars competing for top place in the general classification. The outright winner was not expected to cross the line until between six and half-past in the evening. For the tired spectator there was just the possibility of an hour or two's sleep.

But before there was time to finish breakfast news began to filter in from observers who had gone out to watch the cars on the early section of the route. Moss had passed a car on the tight bend after Lonato and held the Mercedes in a spectacular slide. Taruffi was driving with genius and taking an individual line through the corners which seemed to indicate that he was the only man who had the confidence to tackle them in the correct way. Maglioli was sawing at his steering-wheel with a do or die set to his head. The arm he had injured in practice was worrying him. Fangio was motoring quietly. Experts put forward the theory that he was only getting power from seven out of eight cylinders.

Now the first official results leaked out from the Press Room. Marzotto had averaged 123 m.p.h. to Verona. Castellotti and Taruffi were only just slower. Hermann on the fastest Mercedes had done 120 m.p.h. The quarrels of Capulet and Montagu had become very ancient history in Verona.

Hardly was he through Verona than Marzotto was the victim of a terrifying incident. He was travelling at 170 m.p.h. along a road lined with spectators when one of his tyres threw a tread. Though bared to the canvas the tyre did not burst. Marzotto, with incredible skill, kept the

43

car under control, and brought it to a standstill. But you must not tempt Fate too much. Wisely Marzotto retired from the race and brought his car back to Brescia along the by-roads.

Meanwhile the hurricane swept on through Vicenza, Padua and Ferrara to Ravenna, the first control where drivers had to stop and have their books stamped. For the first 190 miles Castellotti on the 4·4 litre Ferrari had averaged 120 m.p.h. Moss was a little less than two minutes slower. Taruffi, Hermann, Kling and Maglioli followed in that order.

On the fast coastal stretch from Ravenna to Pescara, 200 miles farther on, Castellotti's wild driving took toll of his tyres and engine. He had been using the whole width of the road at corners, frequently raising clouds of dust and showers of stones. Following behind him Moss never knew whether the Italian had crashed or not. Soon after reaching Pescara Castellotti retired from the fray.

At the Pescara control Taruffi's Ferrari was in the lead. Moss was only 15 seconds slower and behind came the remaining three Mercedes in a solid phalanx—Hermann, Kling, Fangio. Their times were:

1.	Taruffi	Ferrari	3:18:58
2.	Moss	Mercedes	3:19:13
3.	Hermann	Mercedes	3:21:11
4.	Kling	Mercedes	3:25:34
5.	Fangio	Mercedes	3:27:18
6.	Maglioli	Ferrari	3:30:33
7.	Perdisa	Maserati	3:31:05
8.	Sighinolfi	Ferrari	3:37:13

Both Ferrari and Mercedes had arranged to refuel at Pescara. Moss filled up with petrol and was away in 28 seconds. Taruffi was at a standstill for more than a minute. The Italian crowd were shouting protests before their hero drove off, but even they did not realise that Moss had gone into the lead at that moment.

Now the first crossing of the Appenines lay ahead, the mountainous section between Pescara and Rome where the average was sure to drop. This was where Taruffi should be able to show his superiority over the British driver. But Moss was a deposer of Kings of the Mountain. Undeterred by the dent his car had suffered when he ran through the straw bales at Pescara he attacked the difficult mountain road with reckless skill. He had acquired the ruthlessness any driver must have who is to take his car at maximum speed through a bend whose unguarded fringes are crowded with spectators, or into a thronged village street where there is only just room to squeeze past. Spectators have forgotten the tragic incident at Bologna in 1938 when twenty people were killed and the race was stopped by order of the Duce. They are prepared to stake their lives on a driver's ability to steer his car on a hair's-breadth.

Before Rome was reached Moss had increased his lead over Taruffi, himself a Roman, to 1 minute 49 seconds. The average was still high, 108 m.p.h. Five hours had passed since the cars left Brescia and they had covered 540 miles. It was not yet lunchtime.

In assessing this achievement it must be remembered that these roads have not by any means fast straight highways. In most places the surface is very bumpy—more so than even secondary roads in England. Except for the sections by the Adriatic and after Bologna the route is constantly twisting. Frequently the camber falls away steeply at the edges and almost all the time there are rows of stout trees waiting to clout any car that slides off. They are the sort of roads on which you would consider it very good going to maintain an average of 40 m.p.h.

Rome is the turning point of the race and the most important control. A long-standing legend of the Mille Miglia states that the leader at Rome never wins. In past years the fate of Taruffi and Kling had given the legend strength.

The order now was:

1.	Moss	Mercedes	5:03:05
2.	Taruffi	Ferrari	5:04:54
3.	Hermann	Mercedes	5:07:06
4.	Kling	Mercedes	Time not given
5.	Fangio	Mercedes	5:14:10
6.	Perdisa	Maserati	5:19:01
7.	Maglioli	Ferrari	5:21:50
8.	Sighinolfi	Ferrari	5:33:23

The Mercedes plan was to refuel again at Rome and to change tyres if necessary. The time allowed by Neubauer for this operation was 1 minute 40 seconds. Moss was at a standstill for only one minute and in that space his tank was filled with petrol and the rear tyres changed. He had barely time to nip into the little tent which had been thoughtfully provided as part of the Mercedes service.

Now he was on the homeward road, but there were still 450 miles to go.

Within a matter of minutes the character of the race had suffered a dramatic change. A little way out of Rome Karl Kling, driving at the very limit of his powers in a bid to gain the lead, rounded a bend to find that its whole shape was altered. The spectators had surged forward to follow the progress of the car in front of him. The sudden spectacle of the low German car with its gaping maw made the spectators panic. One of them tried to cross the road. Swerving to avoid him, Kling lost control of his car which somersaulted off the road. He was lucky to escape with a

46

couple of broken ribs, but desperately unlucky to end his Mille Miglia thus after such careful preparation.

Even more bitter was the lot of Taruffi. At Viterbo, almost the exact spot where trouble with his oil tank had put him out the year before, he was eliminated by a fractured oil pipe. That was the end of the Ferrari challenge and three Mercedes were left in command of the race. The question now in the minds of British supporters was: could Moss maintain his lead with Hermann and Fangio so close on his heels?

Close on his heels is the wrong term, for in fact Fangio was still ahead of Moss on the road. He reached the Florence control a few minutes before Moss and stopped. The bonnet was raised and the low car was surrounded by Mercedes mechanics. It was still stationary when Moss came down the street and swung across the tramlines towards the control. His wheels never stopped rolling as his passenger held out his book for stamping, and he never knew that he had gone past Fangio. Now the Futa and Raticosa Pass lay ahead of the big cars and of these only Hermann's Mercedes was on the road in front of him.

Twenty miles later a stone pierced Hermann's petrol tank and he was out of the running. Pursuing an imaginary Fangio and with an imaginary Taruffi on his tail Moss swept up the Futa Pass in a series of controlled slides. Rubber shed from hundreds of tyres and tar melted by the scorching sun had made the road as slippery as a skating rink. Yet Moss's time from Florence to Bologna was $7\frac{1}{2}$ minutes better than that recorded by Bracco in his famous effort of 1952.

At the Bologna control Geier pushed into the car a paper which gave the race order: Moss, Fangio, Maglioli. But in the excitement it slipped down out of sight. Moss and Jenkinson started off on the flat-out two hundred mile dash back to Brescia at ever-increased speed. Their first indication that they were in the lead came as they accelerated away from the awkwardly cambered bend in Cremona. On the right of the road two unmistakably British figures in blue blazers with shiny buttons made certain rude but jubilant signals. Moss waved both hands and nearly stood up in his seat. Then he put his foot down. So far from coasting to the finish as one English newspaper reported, he averaged 124 m.p.h., over the Cremona, Mantua, Brescia triangle and carried off the Gran Premio Nuvolari. During the long final stretch the Mercedes was cruising at 170 m.p.h., for miles on end, its engine turning at 7,500 revolutions per minute. To Moss's expert ear the power unit sounded perfectly happy—and so it was.

In the Viale Rebuffone the waiting multitude had been electrified by the news that Moss was approaching Brescia at twenty-past five, almost an hour sooner than he was expected. Still uncertain whether he had won, he brought the Mercedes round the final bend at the maximum possible speed, flicked it out of an incipent slide and went for the finishing line at full throttle. With headlights blazing and horns going full blast the British driver took the chequered flag at 150 m.p.h.

Between an early breakfast and late tea he had covered 1,000 miles of very mixed roads. His average for the ten hours odd had been 98 m.p.h. He had raised the race speed by more than any other previous winner and broken the long succession of Italian successes. Fangio was over half an hour behind and Maglioli on the first Ferrari was still eighty miles away.

Such are the bare facts of the 1955 Mille Miglia, but how little they tell of the six hundred dramas that were enacted during the long night and the sunny day. What about Ferrante Viola, the miller of Lonato, who won undying

48

fame in his native village when he confounded his critics and finished first in his class? What about Ron Flockhart, who in his first Mille Miglia had to deal with the worst conditions it could produce? To the Italian crowd the race was over when Taruffi, the backmarker, had passed. They swarmed over the roads and streets. Fighting to maintain an average of 80 m.p.h. in hopeless conditions, Flockhart swerved to avoid a dog. His car slid, went through a bridge backwards, and toppled upside down into the river beneath, trapping its driver in the cockpit. He managed to wriggle out under the side and come to the surface. The hands of penitent Italians dragged him up the bank and plied him well with brandy both inside and out. Flockhart's dormant Presbyterian instincts only rebelled when they tried to take him to their chapel to light a candle in thanks for his delivery.

What of the little Isettas which averaged 50 m.p.h. to Rome? What of John Heath, who finished high in the general classification in the car which had brought him and his wife on a spring tour of Italy?

Luckily, however, we have the inside story of the winner's drive, for Stirling Moss's passenger was Denis Jenkinson, the Foreign Correspondent of *Motor Sport*. The long article he wrote for his magazine was perhaps the greatest scoop of motoring journalism and his editor has generously allowed the following impressions to be reproduced.

" Thirty seconds before 7.22 a.m. Moss started the engine and then the flag fell and we were off with a surge of acceleration and up to peak revs. in first, second and third gears, weaving our way through the vast crowds lining the sides of the road. Had we not been along this same road three times already in an S L R amid the hurly-burly of morning traffic, I should have been thoroughly frightened, but now, with the roads clear ahead of us, I thought Moss could really get down to some uninterrupted motoring. We had the sun shining full in our eyes, which made navigating difficult, but I had written the notes over and over again and gone over the route in my imagination so many times that I almost knew it by heart. One of the first signals was to take a gentle S-bend through a village on full throttle in fourth gear, and as Moss did this, being quite unable to see the road for more than 100 yards ahead, I settled down to the job, confident that our scientific method of equalling the Italians' ability at open road racing was going to work. At no time before the race did we ever contemplate getting into the lead, for we fully expected Fangio to set the pace, with Kling determined to win at all costs, so we were out for a third place and to beat all the Ferraris. Barely 10 miles after the start we saw a red speck in front of us and had soon nipped by on a left-hand curve. It was 720, Pinzero, number 721 being a non-starter. By my right hand was a small grab rail and a horn button; the steering was on the left of the cockpit, by the way, and this button not only blew the horn, but also flashed the lights, so that while I played a fanfare on this Moss placed the car for overtaking other competitors. My direction indications I was giving with my left hand, so what with turning the map roller and feeding Moss with sucking sweets there was never a dull moment. The car was really going well now, and on the straights to Verona we were getting 7,500 in top gear, a speed of 274 k.p.h., or as close to 170 m.p.h. as one could wish to travel. On some of these long straights our navigation system was paying handsomely, for we could keep at 170 m.p.h. over blind brows, even when overtaking slower cars, Moss sure in the knowledge that all he had to do was to concentrate on keeping the car on the road and travelling as fast as possible. This in itself was more than enough, but he was sitting back in his usual relaxed position, making no apparent effort, until some corners were reached when the speed at which he controlled slides, winding the wheel from right to left and back again, showed that his superb reflexes and judgment were on top of their form.

" Cruising at maximum speed, we seemed to spend most of the time between Verona and Vicenza passing Austin. Healeys that could not have been doing much more than 115 m.p.h., and with flashing lights, horn blowing and a wave of the hand, we went by as though they were touring. Approaching Padova Moss pointed behind and I looked round to see a Ferrari gaining on us rapidly, and with a grimace of disgust at one another we realised it was Castellotti. The Mercedes-Benz was giving all it had, and Moss was driving hard but taking no risks, letting the car slide just so far on the corners and no more. Entering the main street of Padova at 150 m.p.h., we braked for the right-angle bend at the end, and suddenly I realised that Moss was beginning to work furiously on the steering-wheel, for we were arriving at the corner much too fast and it seemed doubtful whether we could stop in time. I sat fascinated, watching Moss working away to keep control, and I was so intrigued to follow his every action and live every inch of the way with him, that I completely forgot to be scared. With the wheels almost on locking-point he kept the car straight to the last possible fraction of a second, making no attempt to get round the corner, for that would have meant a complete spin and then anything could happen. Just when it seemed we must go head-on into the straw bales Moss got the speed low enough to risk letting go the brakes and try taking the corner, and as the front of the car slid over the dry road we went *bump*! into the bales with our left-hand front corner, bounced off into the middle of the road and, as the car was then pointing in the right direction, Moss selected bottom gear and opened out again.

51

"All this time Castellotti was right behind us, and as we bounced off the bales he nipped by us, grinning over his shoulder. As we set off after him, I gave Moss a little handclap of appreciation for showing me just how a really great driver acts in a difficult situation.

"Through Padova we followed the 4·4 litre Ferrari and on acceleration we could not hold it, but the Italian was driving like a maniac, sliding all the corners, using the pavements and the loose edges of the road. Round a particularly dodgy left-hand bend on the outskirts of the town I warned Moss and then watched Castellotti sorting out his Ferrari, the front wheels on full under-steer, with the inside one off the ground, and rubber pouring off the rear-tyres, leaving great wide marks on the road. This was indeed motor racing from the best possible position, and beside me was a quiet, calm young man who was following the Ferrari at a discreet distance, ready for any emergency. Out of the town we joined an incredibly fast stretch of road straight for many miles, and we started alongside the Ferrari in bottom gear, but try as the Mercedes-Benz did the red car just drew away from us, and once more Moss and I exchanged very puzzled looks. By the time we had reached our maximum speed the Ferrari was over 200 yards ahead, and then it remained there, the gap being unaltered along the whole length of the straight. At the cut-off point at the end we gained considerably, both from the fact that we knew exactly when the following left-hand corner was approaching and also from slightly superior brakes. More full-throttle running saw us keeping the Ferrari in sight, and then as we approached a small town we saw Castellotti nip past another Ferrari and we realised we were going to have to follow through the streets until there was room to pass. It was number 714, Carini, so soon, and this encouraged Moss to run right round the outside of the Ferrari, on a right-hand curve, confident from my signals that the road would not suddenly turn left. This very brief delay had let Castellotti get away from us but he was not completely out of sight. Out on the open roads he was driving so near the limit that on every corner he was using the gravel and rough stuff on the edges of the road. This sent up a huge cloud of dust, and we could never be sure whether or not we were going to enter it to find the Ferrari sideways across the road, or bouncing off the banks and trees, for this sort of hazard a scientific route-navigating method could not cope with. Wisely, Moss eased back a little and the Ferrari got ahead of us sufficiently to let the dust clouds settle.

" Approaching the Ravenna control I took the route-card board from its holder, held it up for Moss to see, bang went the rubber stamp, and we were off without actually coming to rest. Just beyond the control were a row of pits and there was 723, Castellotti's Ferrari, having some tyre changes, which was not surprising in view of the way he had been driving.

" Moss accelerated hard round the next corner and we twisted our way through the streets of Ravenna, nearly collecting an archway in the process, and then out on the fast winding road to Forli. Our time to Ravenna had been well above the old record but Castellotti had got there before us and we had no idea how Taruffi and the others behind us were doing.

" Now the calm, blue Adriatic sea appeared on our left and we were on the long coastal straights, taking blind brows, and equally blind bridges at our full 170 m.p.h., and I chuckled to myself as I realised that Moss was not lifting his foot as he had threatened. We were beginning to pass earlier numbers very frequently now, among them some two-litre Triumphs running in convoy, and various saloons, with still numerous signs of the telling pace, a wrecked

53

Giulietta on the right, a 1,100 c.c. Fiat on the left, a Ferrari
coupé almost battered beyond recognition and a Renault
that had been rolled up into a ball.

" It was a long way down to the next control point at
Pescara, and we settled down to cruising at our maximum
speed, the car giving no impression at all of how fast it was
travelling. On one straight, lined with trees, we had marked
down a bump in the road as being ' flat-out ' only if the
road was dry. It was, so I gave the appropriate signal and
with 7,500 r.p.m., in fifth gear on the tachometer we took
off, for we had made an error in our estimation of the
severity of the hump. For a measurable amount of time the
vibro-massage that you get sitting in a 300 S L R at that
speed suddenly ceased, and there was time for us to look
at each other with raised eyebrows before we landed again.
Even had we been in the air for only one second we should
have travelled some 200 feet through the air, and I
estimated the ' duration of flight ' at something more than
one second. The road was dead straight and the Mercedes-
Benz made a perfect fourpoint landing and I thankfully
praised the driver that he didn't move the steering-wheel a
fraction of an inch, for that would have been our end.
With the heat of the sun and the long straights we had been
getting into a complacent stupor, but this little ' moment '
brought us back to reality and we were fully on the job
when we approached Pescara. Over the level crossing we
went, faster than we had ever done in practice, and the
car skated right across the road, with all four wheels sliding,
and I was sure we were going to write-off some of the petrol
pumps by the roadside, but somehow ' the boy ' got control
again and we merely brushed some straw bales and then
braked heavily to a stop for the second control stamp. Just
beyond the control line we saw engineer Werner holding a
blue flag bearing the Mercedes-Benz star and as we stopped

everything happened at once. Some 18 gallons of fuel went in from a gravity tank, just sufficient to get us to our main stop at Rome, the windscreen was cleaned for it was thick with dead flies, a hand gave me a small sheet of paper, while another gave me a slice of orange and a peeled banana, someone else was looking at the tyres and Moss still had the engine running. On the paper was written, ' Taruffi, Moss 15 seconds, Hermann, Kling, Fangio.' and their times; I had just yelled ' Second, 15 seconds behind Taruffi,' when I saw a uniformed arm trying to switch off the ignition. I recognised an interfering police arm and gave it a thump, and as I did so, Moss crunched in bottom gear and we accelerated away as hard as we could go. What seemed like an age was actually only 28 seconds!

" Over the bridge we went, sharp right and then up one of the side turnings of Pescara towards the station, where we were to turn right again. There was a blue Gordini just going round the corner and then I saw that we were over-shooting and with locked wheels we slid straight on, *bang* into the straw bales. I just had time to hope there was nothing solid behind the wall of bales when the air was full of flying straw and we were on the pavement. Moss quickly selected bottom gear and without stopping he drove along the pavement behind the bales, until he could bounce down off the kerb and continue on his way, passing the Gordini in the process. As we went up through the gears on the long straight out of Pescara, I kept an eye on the water temperature gauge, for that clonk certainly creased the front of the car, and may have damaged the radiator, or filled the intake with straw, but all seemed well, the temperature was still remaining constant. There followed three completely blind brows in quick succession and we took these at full speed, the effect being rather like a switch-back at a fair, and then we wound and twisted our way

along the barren valley between the rocky mountain sides
to Popoli where a Bailey Bridge still serves to cross a river.
Along this valley I saw the strange sight of about fifty robed
monks with shining bald pates, standing on a high mound
and waving to us as we went by with a noise sufficient to
wake the devil himself.

" We certainly were not wasting any seconds anywhere
and Moss was driving absolutely magnificently, right on the
limit of adhesion all the time, and more often than not over
the limit, in that awe-inspiring narrow margin that you
enter just before you have a crash, or those few yards of
momentary terror you have on ice just before you go in the
ditch. This masterly handling was no fluke, he was doing
it deliberately, his extra special senses and reflexes allowing
him to go that much closer to the absolute limit than the
average racing driver and way beyond the possibilities of
normal mortals like you or me.

" The last six miles into the Rome control were an
absolute nightmare; there were no corners that needed
signals, and we would normally have done 150–160 m.p.h.,
but the crowds of spectators were so thick that we just could
not see the road, and the surface being bumpy Moss dared
not drive much over 130 m.p.h., for there was barely room
for two cars abreast. It seemed that the whole of Rome
was out to watch the race, and all oblivious of the danger
of a high-speed racing car. While I blew the horn and
flashed the lights Moss swerved the car from side to side
and this had the effect of making those on the very edge
leap hastily backwards, thus giving us a little more room.
The last mile into the control was better organised and I was
able to show Moss the control card, point backwards at the
fuel tank and also at the fibre disc wired to the steering-
column which had to be punched at this control. ' Bang '
went the stamp and we then drew into the Mercedes-Benz

pit and switched off the engine; this was our first real stop since leaving Brescia nearly 3½ hours ago.

" As we stopped Moss leapt out to relieve himself, I felt the car rise up on the jacks and heard the rear hub nuts being beaten off, the windscreen was cleaned and a welcome shower of water sprinkled over me, for I was very hot, very tired, very dirty, oily and sweaty and must have looked a horrible sight to spectators. Bump went the car as it was dropped down off the jacks, and with a lithe bound Moss was into the driving-seat again and as we took the hairpin after the control I managed to yell in his ear ' First by more than one minute from Taruffi ' and then the noise of the exhaust and wind prevented any further words. On the next bend we saw a silver Mercedes-Benz number 701, well off the road among the trees and badly wrecked. We knew it was Kling and exhanged long faces with each other, wondering how badly hurt he was, but this had no effect on Moss and he now began to put everything he knew into his driving. We sped on our way through Viterbo sliding this way and that, leaving the ground on more occasions than I can remember. Up the Radicofani Pass we stormed and the way the car leapt and slithered about would have really frightened me had I not already had a lot of experience of its capabilities and of the skill of Stirling Moss; as it was I sat there and revelled in the glorious feeling of really fast motoring.

" Over the top of the pass we swept past a saloon car competitor, into a downhill right-hand bend followed by a sharp left-hander. Now, previous to this Moss had been pointing to the front of the car and indicating that a brake was beginning to grab on occasions, and this was one of them. Without any warning the car spun and there was just time to think what a desolated part of Italy in which to crash, when I realised that we had almost stopped in our own length and were sliding gently into the ditch to land with a crunch that dented the tail.

" ' This is all right,' I thought. ' We can probably push it out of this one.'

" I was about to start getting out when Moss selected bottom gear and we drove out—lucky indeed! Before we could point the car in the right direction we had to make two reverses and as we accelerated away down the mountain-side I fiddled about putting the safety catch back on the reverse position of the gear-gate, while we poked our tongues out at each other in mutual derision.

" On the winding road from Siena to Florence the heat, fumes and noise were becoming almost unbearable, but I gave myself renewed energy by looking at Stirling Moss who was sitting beside me, completely relaxed, working away at the steering as if we had only just left Brescia instead of having been driving for nearly 700 miles under a blazing sun. When we approached one corner some women got up and fled with looks of terror on their faces, for the battered Mercedes-Benz, dirty and oil-stained and making as much noise as a Grand Prix car, with two sweaty, dirty, oil-stained figures behind the windscreen, must have looked terrifying to peaceful peasants, as it entered the corner in a full four-wheel slide.

" The approaches of Florence were almost back-breaking as we bounced and leapt over the badly maintained roads and across the tramlines. At speeds of up to 120–130 m.p.h. we went through the streets of Florence, over the great river bridge, broadside across a square, across more tramlines and into the control point. Now Moss had really got the bit between his teeth, nothing was going to stop him winning this race, I felt; he had a rather special look of concentration on his face and I knew that one of his greatest ambitions was to do the section Florence-Bologna in under one hour.

58

" He left Florence, as though at the start of a Grand Prix. I took a firm grip of the ' struggling bar,' for he was going to need all the room possible for his whirling arms and for stirring the gear lever about. Up into the mountains we screamed, occasionally passing other cars, such as 1900 Alfa-Romeos, 1,100 Fiats and some small sports cars. Little did we know that we had the race in our pocket for Taruffi had retired by this time with a broken oil pump and Fangio was stopped in Florence repairing an injection pipe. At the top of the Futa Pass there were enormous crowds all waving excitedly and on numerous occasions Moss nearly lost the car completely as we hit patches of melted tar, coated with oil and rubber from all the other competitors in front of us and for nearly a mile he had to ease off, the road was so tricky.

" I marvelled that anyone could drive so furiously for such a long time, for it was now well into the Sunday afternoon. On we went, up and over the Raticosa Pass, plunging down the other side in one long series of slides that to me felt completely uncontrolled but to Moss were obviously intentional. However, there was one particular one which was not intentional and by sheer good fortune the stone parapet on the outside of the corner stepped back just in time. On another part of the Raticosa amid great crowds of people we saw an enormous fat man in the road, leaping up and down with delight; it was the happy body-builder of the Maserati racing department, and a good friend of Stirling's, and we waved back to him.

" Down off the mountains we raced, into the broiling heat of the afternoon along the dusty tramlined road with hordes of spectators on both sides, but here beautifully controlled, so that we went into Bologna at close on 150 m.p.h. The hard part was now over, but Moss did not relax, for it had now occurred to him that it was possible to get back to

Brescia in the round ten hours, which would make the race average 100 m.p.h. Up the long fast straights through Modena, Reggio Emilia and Parma we went, not wasting a second anywhere, cruising at a continuous 170 m.p.h., cutting off only where I indicated corners, or bumpy hill-brows. Through Cremona we went and now we were on the last leg of the course, there being a special prize and the Nuvolari Cup for the fastest speed from Cremona to Brescia. Although the road lay straight for most of the way, there were more than six villages to traverse, as well as the final route card stamp to get in the town of Mantova. In one village, less than 50 miles from the finish, we had an enormous slide on some melted tar and for a moment I thought we would hit a concrete wall, but with that absurdly calm manner of his, Moss tweaked the wheel this way and that, and caught the car just in time, and with his foot hard down we went on our way as if nothing had happened. The final miles into Brescia were sheer joy, the engine was singing round on full power, and after we had passed our final direction indication I put my roller-map away and thought:

" ' If it blows to pieces now, we can carry it the rest of the way.'

" The last corner into the finishing area was taken in a long slide with the power and noise full on and we crossed the finishing line at well over 100 m.p.h., still not knowing that we had made motor-racing history, but happy and contented at having completed the whole race and done our best.

" It was with a justified feeling of elation that I lay in a hot bath, for I had had the unique experience of being with Stirling Moss throughout his epic drive, sitting beside him while he worked as I have never seen anyone work before in my life, and harder and longer than I ever thought it possible for a human being to do."

60

OFFICIAL RESULTS

Number of starters: 533
Number of finishers: 240

Place Driver	Car	Time	Average in K.P.H.	Remarks
1. Moss	Mercedes	10.07.48	157·650	3 litre 300 S L R ⎰ Also 1st,
2. Fangio	Mercedes	10.39.33		3 litre 300 S L R ⎱ 2nd, 3rd, in over 2,000 c.c. class.
3. Maglioli	Ferrari	10.52.47		
4. Giardini	Maserati	11.15.32	141·843	Winner Sports Class up to 2,000 c.c.
5. Fitch	Mercedes	11.29.21	139	Winner Gran Turismo Class over 1,300 c.c.
6. Sighinolfi	Ferrari	11.33.27		4th in over 2,000 Sports Class.
7. Gendebien	Mercedes	11.36.00	131·570	2nd in Gran Turismo Class over 1,300 c.c.
8. Seidel	Porsche	12.08.17	131·570	Winner Sports Class up to 1,500 c.c.
9. Bellucci	Maserati	12.09.10		2nd Sports class up to 2,000 c.c.
10. Casella	Mercedes	12.11.15		3rd in Gran Turismo over 1,300 c.c.
11. Abecassis	Austin-Healey	12.21.43		First British car. 5th in over 2,000 c.c. Sports Class

OTHER CLASS WINNERS

21. Frankenberg	Porsche	12.58.39	123·059	Winner Sports Class up to 1,300 c.c.
25. Bourillot	Osca	13.01.21	122·63	Winner Sports Class up to 1,100 c.c.
36. Storez	D.B.	13.21.03	119·618	Winner Sports Class up to 750 c.c.
55. Mandrini	Fiat	13.48.12		Winner Special series 750-1,300 c.c.
82. Viola	Fiat	14.32.50		Winner Gran Turismo to 1,100 c.c.
92. Galtier	Renault	14.44.59		Winner Special series up to 750 c.c. First car to finish.

OTHER BRITISH CARS AND DRIVERS TO FINISH

35. Macklin	Austin-Healey	13.19.25	8th in Sports Class over 2,000 c.c.
40. Heath	Jaguar	13.24.27	
59. Brooke	Triumph	13.54.52	
87. Verilli	Austin-Healey	14.38.52	Italian driver of British car.

61

CHAPTER THREE

ASCARI'S LAST RACE

European Grand Prix. Monaco. 22 May

EVERY YEAR one of the national Grands Prix also carries the title of European Grand Prix. This year the honour was bestowed on the contest to be organised in the tiny Principality of Monaco. But the 1955 event will be remembered by all who were in Monte Carlo on Sunday, May 22nd, as Alberto Ascari's race.

There is no item on the International Motor Racing Calendar which offers a more striking contrast to the Mille Miglia. In the first place Monaco was to be a Formula One event and the cars entered were pure-bred racers. The circuit was a fraction less than two miles round and had to be covered 100 times to make the distance worthy of a Grand Epreuve. Owing to the narrowness of the course and the danger of multiple crashes only twenty cars were to be accepted for the race itself. The setting consisted of the streets, avenues and promenade of the Principality of Monaco.

Monaco is still an independent state. Since the twelfth century it has been ruled by the Grimaldi family. The present ruler, His Serene Highness Prince Rainier III, looks down upon his princedom from the lofty splendour of a feudal castle, but he exercises his power democratically through a Minister of State and a National Council.

62

Although there is no customs barrier between France and
the Principality, Monaco has its own Army, its own Police,
its own postage stamps and coinage. Its inhabitants do not
pay Income Tax nor Death Duties. Most of all it makes
its own laws. It was this legal independence which allowed
the first gambling Casino outside Germany to be opened;
a shrewd business move, for it rapidly made Monaco a
magnet for the wealthy classes of all nations. This same
legal independence makes it possible for the Authorities to
close the streets of a thriving city for two mornings and an
afternoon of practice and for almost the whole of the Sunday
on which the race is run.

The French call this race " La Course dans la Cité."
Racing drivers have other names for it. The setting is one
which only the naked eye can grasp; no film or cinema
picture can embrace the 360 degree panorama. In the
centre is the natural deep anchorage which decided the
Saracens to build their citadel above the bay, guarded to
left and right by steep, cliff-like slopes. Here a warship
may lie at anchor a stone's throw from the balcony windows,
and the pleasure yachts of millionaires are lined up like
prize steers in a market pen with their tails tied to the
harbour wall. Behind, tier upon tier in a great amphitheatre, rise the hotels and palaces, the snow-white blocks
of luxury flats, the terraced villas and the mountains. To
one side you look along the French coast towards the
pleasure beaches of Nice and Cannes, and on the other
towards Cap Martin and the Italian Riviera. Before you
lies the Mediterranean, glittering in the sun under an
unbroken blue sky. On the hill of Monte Carlo the
fabled Casino, shining with fresh paint and girt by exotic
herbage, leaves you in no doubt that it holds the con-
trolling interest in this city whose industry is the life of
luxury.

63

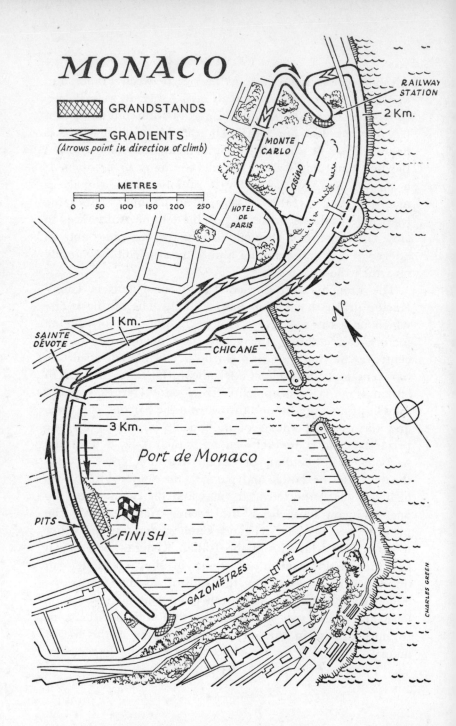

Monaco. Ascari checks the seat adjustment of his Lancia   (*Photo Rutherford*)

Monaco. A few seconds after the start. Fangio (2) and Moss (6) have beaten
Castellotti (30) and Ascari (26) to the first hairpin   (*Photo Erdé, Monte-Carlo*)

Monaco. Trintignant aboard the winning Ferrari negotiates the Virage des Gazomètres   *(Photo Cahier)*

Monaco. A typical study of the leading Mercedes drivers, Fangio in a well defined four-wheel drift   *(Photo Associated Press)*

The port of Monaco is an almost perfect square, land-locked on three sides, and edged with a broad promenade. The Grand Prix circuit begins in the middle of the central strip, the Quai Albert Premier. Here on the tree-lined concrete walk, usually barred to wheeled traffic, are the pits and start line. Ahead lie two miles of streets bordered by kerbstones, monumental balustrades, house walls, even the deep waters of the harbour itself. It is not surprising then that this circuit is the slowest on the calendar. The lap record was established by Rudolf Carracciola in 1937 on a supercharged Mercedes of 5·6 litres developing well over 600 brake horse power. His speed was a shade over 67 m.p.h.

The 1955 race was the 13th in a series which began in 1929. It was run every year until 1937, but since the war it had only been organised in 1948, '50 and '52. In the early days it was dominated by Bugatti and Alfa-Romeo until the coming of the all-conquering Mercedes. The German firm scored wins in '35, '36 and secured the first three places in 1937. Since the war Maserati, Alfa-Romeo and Ferrari had each respectively achieved a win.

Monaco is notorious for the strain it exerts on both car and driver, and for its capacity to dash the hopes of those who see victory within sight. Its history has been marked by drama and tragedy. Twice there have been multiple crashes. In 1936 the race started in a torrential downpour. Worse still, one of the cars deposited some oil on the approach to the artificial corner constructed on the Promenade. On the second lap the leaders, Carracciola and Nuvolari, managed to waltz through, but the next five cars crashed to form a hopeless jumble, virtually blocking the road. By a miracle none of the drivers was hurt. Some laps later Fagioli spun on the same patch of oil and crashed.

He escaped on that occasion but his name was on the Promenade wall, for he was killed when he hit it again fifteen years later during practice for the 1952 race. In 1950 another multiple crash occurred on the very first lap, again on the Promenade. Farina spun wildly and was rammed by Gonzalez following close behind. The tight-bunched field had not a chance of stopping and half of the cars retired with damage of varying degrees. Fangio, who was leading, noticed in his mirror that the road behind was empty and was at a loss to understand how he had got so far ahead. Just as he was about to turn on to the Promenade some little cell in his brain reminded him of a photograph of the 1936 incident which he had seen the day before. He slowed down, rounded the next corner cautiously, and found the road littered with wrecked cars.

Monaco was Round Two in the Formula One Championship. Round One, the Argentine Grand Prix, had been decisively won by Fangio for Mercedes. Some there were who pointed out that Mercedes had won four out of the six Grandes Epreuves for which they had entered in 1954, and suggested that German invincibility would again kill Formula One racing. The first two practice sessions had confirmed Mercedes as favourites, although they had also suffered a set-back. Fangio had smashed Carracciola's long standing record by no less than 5 seconds. His time of 1 minute 41 1/10th seconds was a good 10 seconds better than that recorded previously by any unsupercharged car and represented a mean speed of 70 m.p.h. On the other hand Hermann had touched one of the murderous kerb-stones near the Casino and was lucky to be alive. His car had buried its nose between the props of a stone balustrade and brought Hermann to within a foot of solid concrete. His injuries were slight, but enough to keep him out of the

EUROPEAN GRAND PRIX

ENTRY LIST

Driver				Car
Fangio	..	..	..	Mercedes
Hermann	..	..	..	Mercedes
Moss ..	..	..	..	Mercedes
Manzon	..	..	..	Gordini
Pollet	..	..	..	Gordini
Bayol ..	..	..	..	Gordini
Rosier	..	..	..	Maserati
Simon	..	..	..	Maserati
Hawthorn	..	..	..	Vanwall
Wharton	..	..	..	Vanwall
Macklin	..	..	..	Maserati
Whiteaway	..	..	..	H.W.M.
Ascari	..	..	..	Lancia
Villoresi	..	..	..	Lancia
Castellotti	..	..	..	Lancia
Chiron	..	..	..	Lancia
Behra	..	..	..	Maserati
Mieres	..	..	..	Maserati
Musso	..	..	..	Maserati
Perdisa	..	..	..	Maserati
Farina	..	..	..	Ferrari
Trintignant	..	..	..	Ferrari
Schell	..	..	..	Ferrari
Taruffi	..	..	..	Ferrari

67

race. As Kling was still not fit, the Mercedes driver problem was acute. They decided to call in Simon, already entered privately with a Maserati, to complete their team of three.

Ascari's best speed in the first two practices was a second slower than Fangio's. In a hundred lap race that could mean 1 minute 40 seconds—almost a complete lap. It was not good enough. No man was less ready to accept the theory that Mercedes were invincible than Alberto Ascari, who at the age of thirty-six was at the peak of his form and the idol of all Italy.

Alberto was born in Milan on July 13, 1918. His father was the greatest Italian driver of his day and frequently used to take his son with him to the races in which he competed. A fortnight before Alberto's seventh birthday Antonio Ascari was killed while leading the French Grand Prix at Montléhry. From then on it was Alberto's passion to become a racing driver like his father.

So absorbed was he with this ambition that he twice ran away from school and at the first possible moment bought himself a motor-bike. Like many another champion it was on two wheels that he acquired his instinct for the line of a corner. His first motor race was the 1940 Mille Miglia, and the car he entered was a Ferrari, the very make on which ten years later he was to achieve his greatest successes.

In 1940 he married a Milan girl and they had two children. The boy was named Antonio in memory of his grandfather and the girl was called Patrizia. Ascari was devoted to his family and they continued to live in his native Milan during the years of his fame and glory.

Luigi Villoresi was ten years his senior. He had early

68

recognised the particular gifts of Alberto. After the war it was he who persuaded him to return to racing.

Driving first for Maserati, then for Alfa-Romeo, he impressed everyone by his style and talent. In 1949 he joined the Ferrari team and rapidly rose to supremacy. In 1952 and 1953 he won the title of World Champion. In that first meteoric year of his championship he won the following races:

II Gran Premio di Siracusa
XIII Grand Prix de Pau
Grand Prix de Marseille
Grand Prix d'Europe
XXXIX Grand Prix de l'ACF
VII British Grand Prix
XV Grosser Preis von Deutschland
Grand Prix de Comminges
Grand Prix de la Baule
IV Grote Prijs van Nederland
XXIII Gran Premio d'Italia

When Lancia decided to develop a new Grand Prix car it was essential for them to obtain the services of a really good driver. They made Ascari an offer generous enough to induce him to leave Ferrari. He drove and tested the new Lancia until it was ready to make its first appearance in the 1954 Spanish Grand Prix. This inevitably meant that he was prevented from competing in most of the 1954 races. In fact his only victory that year was the Mille Miglia.

Now at the beginning of this new season the Lancia was ready and Ascari was eager to come to grips with Fangio and if possible win back his championship.

Ascari as a man was modest and sincere. Those who moved around him in the racing world liked him for his friendly joviality. He was always ready to acknowledge the greetings of admirers he did not know from Adam, and to recognise the important contribution his mechanics made to his success. In appearance he was very Italian, with his long Roman nose, flashing eyes and teeth and jet black hair brushed straight back.

Two of his characteristics used to make his friends smile. One was the complicated hitching up of trousers which went on before he stepped into his car. Another was his habit, whenever he stopped at his pit, of pouring the second half of his iced drink down the back of his neck. His lucky charm was his blue helmet. He only drove without it once.

In a racing car with his helmet square on his head and huge goggles covering the upper part of his face he was a ruthless figure. He was not a relaxed driver. With his mouth set and his eyes concentrated he seemed to whip his car along and his sensitive hands constantly manipulated the steering-wheel. When he was really in a hurry he took his bends in a series of dicey jerks rather than in one controlled slide. His policy was to get in front from the start of a race and stay there. To have Ascari on your tail was a truly unnerving experience.

When the cars collected for final practice on the empty Promenade at 5.45 on Saturday morning there was an air of purpose about the Lancia pits. Their four cars were lined up in good time and sixteen mechanics bustled around them. Mercedes seemed more confident. No one tampered with the silver cars as they waited for word that the course was open.

Even at this hour there was a good crowd round the circuit. The illusions of anyone in Monte Carlo who had hoped to sleep late that morning were soon shattered. All along the line mechanics were inserting the splines of portable starters and bringing the engines to life. They had to be well warmed up before racing plugs were fitted. The din echoed across the still water and down the empty streets. It was obvious from Ascari's manner that he meant business. He was very self-contained and thoughtful as he opened up the attaché case in which he carried his racing gear and carefully fitted on goggles, ear plugs, gloves and helmet. When the course was officially opened his was the first car to pull out in the slanting morning sunlight.

A driver starting round this circuit knows that he has three hundred yards to travel before he reaches the most acute hairpin on any Grand Prix course. It rejoices in the sinister name of Virage des Gazomètres. Here the car has to be brought to a mere crawl of 30 m.p.h., and full lock put on. Too early acceleration will only cause your tail to break away. Now you're on the Boulevard running parallel to the Promenade. Time for three quick changes up before swinging right on to the long, steep slope of Avenue Monte Carlo. At the top is a sweeping curve to the left which brings you round to the front of the Casino. If you go over the banisters here you'll land on the Promenade eighty feet below. There's a sharp kerbstone surrounding the nice piece of grass in front of the Casino. You miss it if you can and after a brief straight section the road dives to the right like the Big Dipper. Ahead lies the station, but if your brakes are still operating you don't take the train. Instead you grab a lower gear and at the same time keep that brake on, then lock hard over to the left. If there's a car in front you might just lean your nose on its tail to show there's no ill-feeling. The second left-hand swerve is almost as bad as the first. Ahead is the sea. You go down to it on a toboggan and turn sharp right on to the Boulevard Louis III. Here is the one part of the course on which you can achieve speed, though the road continually curves right. Just as you're going nicely you plunge into the tunnel. Above you is the terrace where Henry Cotton used to arrange for wealthy golfers to slam golf balls out to sea. The kerbstone is still there, close to you, grinning in the gloom. Out into the light again, a sudden descent and ahead of you is what they still call the Chicane. It's really a left and right wriggle which transfers you from the Boulevard on to the Promenade running alongside it. It can be taken at over 100 m.p.h., but the sea is right beside you now and a nasty thought is the iron bollards used by the ships for tying up. A brief surge of acceleration to the Virage de la Sainte Dévote. She's the patron saint of Monaco and she has a bump there which lifts your wheels off the ground for an instant just as you go round the corner. Then comes the straight past the pits and the Royal Stand. You get up as much speed as you can before standing on the brakes to deal with the Gazométres.

You've made anything up to thirty gear changes during the lap. That's going to mean 3,000 during the 3-hour race —or one every 3 seconds.

Nothing sensational happened during the first stage of practising. In fact the places in the front row of the starting grid had been allotted on the times recorded in the first practice session. Fangio, Ascari and Moss were already safely there. But something more than that seemed to be at stake. With half an hour to go the Mercedes of Moss and Fangio were at their pits and three Lancias were lined up. Simon was going round and round in an endeavour to master the Mercedes projectile. Chiron was careering along without respite, savouring the delight of blinding unhindered through the streets of his native town.

Then Fangio and Moss pulled their gloves on again and

with a determined set to their heads accelerated away. Just to show that his performance had been no flash in the pan Fangio equalled his own record. Moss was 1½ seconds slower. There was a small difference in the handling qualities of Moss's and Fangio's cars, due to the engine being slightly farther forward on the latter. Moss found that he could clip almost two seconds off his time when he drove the Champion's car. He recorded 1 minute 42 6/10ths. Mercedes Team Manager Neubauer flagged his men in.

Meanwhile Ascari, with an equally determined look on his face, had gone out again in the Lancia. It was soon clear that Ascari was pulling out all the stops, taking his car closer to the balustrades and kerbstones than any other driver. He performed one desperately fast lap and coasted in to his pit. As he climbed out of the car he seemed very happy. He pulled off his helmet and gloves and patted his mechanic on the shoulder. Maybe there had been some awkward moments on the corners but the engine was fine.

Just as practising was closed the loudspeakers announced that Ascari had equalled Fangio's best time.

This feat, achieved before the race even began, had an important moral effect and directly influenced the course of the race. Not only did it effectively demonstrate that the Italians could match the Germans in engineering for speed, but it warned the Mercedes team that they must drive their cars really fast and keep on doing so if Ascari's Lancia was within striking distance.

With practice ended every car except the H.W.M., driven by Whiteaway, had beaten the post-war lap record. Macklin's mount, the Maserati owned by Stirling Moss, was the next slowest and did not qualify. So only one of the four British entries were left.

Best practice times were:

Fangio	Mercedes	1 min.	41 1/10 secs.	111·989 k.p.h.
Ascari	Lancia	1 „	41 1/10 „	111·989 „
Castellotti	Lancia	1 „	42 „	111 „
Behra	Maserati	1 „	42 5/10 „	110·461 „
Moss	Mercedes	1 „	42 6/10 „	110·353 „

The fortunes of Ferrari were at a low ebb, for their best man, Maurice Trintignant, was ninth on the list. He had chosen to drive the older model in preference to the newer, wicked-looking *squalo*. Hawthorn's Vanwall was three places lower, having recorded a time of 1 minute 45 6/10 seconds. The Gordinis with their older engines of 2·475 c.c. were severely outclassed.

Places on the starting grid were therefore allotted as follows:[1]

	MOSS		ASCARI		FANGIO
	Mercedes		Lancia		Mercedes
		BEHRA		CASTELLOTTI	
		Maserati		Lancia	
	MUSSO		VILLORESI		MIERES
	Maserati		Lancia		Maserati
		SIMON		TRINTIGNANT	
		Mercedes		Ferrari	
	MANZON		HAWTHORN		PERDISA
	Gordini		Vanwall		Maserati
		TARUFFI		FARINA	
		Ferrari		Ferrari	
	SCHELL		ROSIER		BAYOL
	Ferrari		Maserati		Gordini
		POLLET		CHIRON	
		Gordini		Lancia	

[1] The most desirable position on the grid is not the centre but the right or left side, depending on the direction of the first corner after the start. It is an advantage to be on the inside at this crucial bend.
  In this, and all subsequent charts of starting grids, the cars may be imagined as moving towards the top of the page.

On the morning of Sunday a multitude flocked into Monaco from all directions, by plane, train, car and bicycle. The sea-front portion of the circuit is overlooked by what must be the biggest amphitheatre in the world. There were stands and enclosures as always. But on the sloping gardens and terraces the people were as thick as flies in the brilliant sunlight, and as race time approached every balcony and roof was occupied. Even the pleasure yachts in the harbour moved closer for a better view.

The silver, red, blue and green cars came along the seafront and lined up ready in front of their pits. The accredited photographers got busy and officials chased unauthorised persons off the track. There came a brief diversion in the shape of Bella Darvi, star of the motor-racing film *Such Men are Dangerous*. When the photographers had done their worst and recorded the tall blonde in a hundred poses around and in the cars the serious business of the day was allowed to proceed.

Prince Rainier arrived with his party and opened proceedings by driving his own green Lancia round the circuit before taking his place in the Royal Stand. Mechanics pushed the cars on to their positions on the grid. The starter marshalled the drivers round him for a minute's talk before they went to their cars. Fangio sat waiting calmly in his cockpit, Moss rinsed his mouth and spat the water out on to the Quai Albert Premier. Ascari gave his pants that characteristic hitch and climbed over the slab side tanks of the Lancia. Here and there an engine started up and soon all twenty of them were thundering. A fine blue smoke shimmered in the sunlight and ordinary conversation became impossible.

Charles Faroux, the grand old man of French racing, stepped out on to the roadway with the starter's flag. The eyes of every driver were on him as he held up one hand with the five fingers extended. One by one he folded them away to mark the final seconds. The din of the engines rose. The flag dropped and the entire field shot away to a perfect start.

For a moment Ascari led the dash towards the Gasometer Hairpin, three hundred yards away. But Fangio and Moss beat him to it and the latter was able to pull over in front to take the acute bend. There was a pause while the cars sorted themselves out miraculously. Then the whole pack came screaming along the other side of the double road, the wild chorus of straining engines echoing back from the houses. Fangio was out in front followed by Moss, Castellotti, Ascari. Away they went up the slope towards Monte Carlo, their helmeted heads just visible above the balustrade where dowager ladies like to pause and admire the view. After the last cars had disappeared behind the Casino everyone's eyes went to the mouth of the tunnel on the road below where they would appear again. The pause was a short one before the string of heads appeared again, moving unbelievably fast. Even across the bay it was possible to recognise the first cars as they twitched through the Chicane on to the water-front—Mercedes, Lancia, Lancia, Mercedes.

They passed the pits in a brief surge up to 140 m.p.h.— Fangio, Castellotti, Ascari, Moss, Behra, Mieres, Manzon, Villoresi, Perdisa, Trintignant. Farina was already pulling in to his pit. He had touched hubs with another car during the busy first lap and thought it wise to change the wheel. The last car had disappeared up Monte Carlo hill before he got going again. During the rest of the race he worked steadily up through the field to finish fourth. There was barely time to speculate on the reasons for his stoppage before the leaders had appeared again, still

close-coupled and with daggers drawn. Moss had passed
Ascari and the order was Mercedes, Lancia, Mercedes,
Lancia. Not until the fifth lap did the British driver
squeeze past Castellotti. A few laps later Ascari got ahead
of his compatriot to set off in grim pursuit of the two
Mercedes.

Before ten laps were completed Fangio had passed the
Gordini driver Pollet, who was tail-end Charlie. Rosier had
retired with a damaged tail-piece, another victim of the
jostles of the first lap. Musso, a much-favoured Maserati
pilota, trailed into his pit. Out came the jack, up went
the two rear wheels, the gear was engaged but no power
came through the transmission. That was one Maserati
out.

With ten laps on the board, Fangio, averaging 105·392
k.p.h., or approximately 66 m.p.h., was five seconds or so
ahead of Moss. About ten seconds behind came a close-
packed group consisting of the two leading Lancias and
Behra's Maserati. The Frenchman, on his home ground,
was all out to repeat his victories at Pau, Bordeaux and Bari.
The Italians had been duelling with each other but now
Ascari was in front of Castellotti. Trintignant in the leading
Ferrari was ninth and the white hope of the British Common-
wealth of Nations, Hawthorn in the Vanwall, was two
places lower.

The race settled down into what seemed to be its pre-
determined shape. Incidents had been few. The Monaco
Gremlin was lying low and biding her time. At the quarter
distance of 25 laps the two Mercedes had a comfortable lead
over Ascari. On his 27th circuit Fangio established the
fastest time recorded during the race. His 1 minute
42 4/10 seconds meant a speed of 66 m.p.h.—still 4 m.p.h.
slower than his practice time. At Neubauer's signal he

eased very slightly and Moss rapidly closed up till he was riding the Champion's tail.

The task of taking a car fast round the winding circuit seemed to be much easier for the Mercedes drivers than for the others. Moss, driving with his relaxed armchair style, even had a hand free as he took the difficult Virage de la Sainte Dévote. He lifted an extended finger to the Marshall who had shown Fangio the blue flag—" A car is about to overtake you "—to indicate that for the moment he was content to stay in second place. Accelerating away from the Hairpin he drew almost level with Fangio and gave him the Italian " *Ciao* " signal with one hand. Then he settled down to business and there came over his face that expression known to many racegoers in Britain—a blend of resolution, mastery, youth and contentment. Continental crowds like Moss. He's a real professional but he takes it all in the right spirit.

With forty laps on the board the prospects of Lancia were less rosy. Behra had given his Maserati the stick and passed Ascari to take third place. Castellotti's brakes needed attention and he had been forced to stop for long enough to drop to ninth. Villoresi was comfortable but not dangerous at eighth and the fifty-four-year-old Louis Chiron was twelfth. Hawthorn was last but two. Soon afterwards he was definitely eliminated with a broken throttle linkage. A danger note had sounded for Mercedes. Simon's car had already retired with unspecified mechanical trouble, a great disappointment for this driver. The Monaco race had been his chance to hit the headlines.

So there we were. The two leading Mercedes had established their superiority and could afford to take things a little more easily. People began to drift away from the side of the track to sit down at the café tables on the waterfront behind the stands. There they could sit and drink in

78

the sunshine, admire the view and at the same time follow the distant cars as they climbed the hill or sped along the Promenade. Many a young gentleman who believed he had come to watch the racing cars found his attention wandering to the ladies of Monte Carlo in their skin-tight slacks and off-the-shoulder blouses.

As the cars approached their half century of laps there came the first hint of drama. Behra's Maserati was distressed by the beating it had been given and had dug its heels in. The volatile Frenchman was suddenly down to eleventh place. Excitement in the Maserati pit. In he came exuding metaphorical steam. Out jumped Behra and kept on jumping. The big Maserati flag went out to stop young Perdisa, circulating hopefully in sixth place. He came in, braking hard, stared in amazement at the pit staff and Behra gesticulating at him to get out of that cockpit quick. Orders is orders. Perdisa jumped out, Behra jumped in and gave the second Maserati the gun. Perdisa shrugged, climbed into the thrashed Maserati, pulled his goggles down and drove away to do the best he could with it. But the Monaco Gremlin liked young Perdisa. It was he and not Behra who figured in third place when the final results came out.

Those who had been keeping a tally of the laps realised that the Mercedes pair were about to notch up their fiftieth lap. They waited for the familiar Fangio-Moss formation to appear. But this time car number 6 came out of the tunnel all by itself. Moss was past the pits and away round the course again before the news came through. Fangio's car had stopped near the station. As he reached for second gear to take the vicious downhill hairpins his transmission broke. Moss narrowly missed the leading car and squeezed by. Fangio returned to the pits by boat to tell the sad story to Neubauer.

So at half distance the winner of the Mille Miglia had a comfortable lead in the Monaco Grand Prix.

1. Moss	Mercedes—1 hr. 24 min. 31 3/10 secs.	
	Average speed: 108·45 k.p.h.	
2. Ascari	Lancia —1 hr. 25 min. 34 9/10 secs.	
3. Trintignant	Ferrari —1 hr. 26 min. 03·5/10 secs.	
4. Mieres	Maserati —1 hr. 26 min. 05 1/10 secs.	
5. Behra	Maserati	
6. Castellotti	Lancia	
7. Villoresi	Lancia	49 laps
8. Farina	Ferrari	
9. Schell	Ferrari	
10. Perdisa	Maserati	48 laps
11. Chiron	Lancia	47 laps
12. Bayol	Gordini	46 laps
13. Pollet	Gordini	40 laps
14. Taruffi	Ferrari	

Between the sixtieth and seventieth laps things began to warm up, literally as well as metaphorically. Mieres made a bid to take third place and momentarily succeeded. Almost immediately he came into the pits and retired with what seemed to be more transmission trouble. Taruffi was having difficulty with the gears of the last Ferrari and handed over to Frere. The race of a thousand corners was taking its toll. Villoresi spun the Lancia on the Square Massenet and did the same trick in front of the Hotel Mirabeau. Castellotti, driving brilliantly, had come up to fourth place again. All the Gordinis except Pollet's had been eliminated and the field had been reduced to the unlucky number of 13.

Moss was within 7 seconds of catching up with Ascari on the seventieth lap and these two were a clear lap ahead of the next four cars. Then the Italian champion initiated one of those attacks which made him World Champion in 1952 and '53. With that distinctive forward thrust of the head

Spa. Neubauer, the Mercedes team manager, flanked by Fangio and
Moss (right)   *(Photo Cahier)*

Spa. Half a mile from the start. Fangio leads, and Castellotti is just
about to be overtaken by Moss   *(Photo Mercedes-Benz)*

Spa.
Farina absorbed in the
negotiation of La Source
(*Photo Cahier*)

he seemed to be urging the Lancia on. The car was a handful as he took it through the bumpy Dévote curve where the wheels left the ground at the crucial moment when he entered the bend. He was quickly correcting incipient slides as he accelerated away.

Gradually he began to pull away from Moss. By the 77th lap he was winning back two or three seconds per lap. A quick calculation showed that if Moss slackened speed by as much as one second per lap Ascari could catch and pass him on the last circuit. The heat and the pace were beginning to tell on both drivers. Moss's face and arms were black with fumes. After two thousand gear changes his right arm was cramped, but the engine still sounded healthy enough. He raised his speed slightly to resist the challenge of the Lancia.

Moss completed his eightieth lap and had only 40 miles to go.

1. Moss	5. Behra
2. Ascari	6. Villoresi
3. Trintignant	7. Farina
4. Castellotti	8. Perdisa

Once again the whole character of the race changed. When Moss appeared along the Promenade the blue fumes of burning oil were pouring from his engine. He swung in towards his pit, his head and shoulders wreathed in smoke.

At that very moment Ascari was on the road just above and going in the opposite direction. He attacked the steep slope of Avenue Monte Carlo and disappeared behind the Casino. Moss had climbed out of his car and the mechanics were loosening the bonnet catches. On his car too the pistons had packed up for the day.

From the back of the stands it was possible to see across the bay to the Chicane. In thirty seconds Ascari's blue

helmet came into view, then the low, red car. It approached
the Chicane very fast—too fast. There was a brief moment
when the Lancia skidded with shrieking tyres, then it
smashed through planking, sandbags and straw bales.
There was a gigantic splash as it hit the water of the bay.
Steam from the hot engine mingled with the dust and
fragments of straw floating in the air. For an agonising
three seconds everyone's breath stopped. Had the driver
been trapped and gone to the bottom with his car? Then
the pale blue helmet appeared bobbing on the surface.
Ascari was hauled into a boat before even the frogmen could
reach him.

So, after all, it was Trintignant and not Ascari who went
through to take the lead. This compact little Frenchman
owns extensive vineyards in the Rhône Valley and takes
part in motor races for pure pleasure. He is neat and
dapper in his dress and his handling of a car has the same
well-tailored, lasting quality as his suits. He had driven a
fast but steady race and seen the successive elimination of
all the eight drivers who had been in front of him at the
end of the tenth lap.

Just to preserve its reputation for last-minute surprises,
the Monaco circuit deluded Behra into spinning on a patch
of oil near the Casino and making the acquaintance, as he
put it, of the décor. With only a few laps to go he was robbed
of third place, having brought Perdisa's Maserati up from
seventh.

In this 1955 European Grand Prix it was the older and
well-tried car that triumphed. The combined onslaught
of the three Italian makes had so discomfited the Germans
that not one Mercedes had survived the ordeal. Herr
Neubauer and his accomplices withdrew to Stuttgart to
meditate upon the Daimler-Benz counterthrust.

Meanwhile the man who had done most to re-establish

Italian prestige was lying in a hospital bed suffering from nothing worse than a broken nose and, not surprisingly, shock.

As Ascari drove up towards the Casino on that fateful eighty-first lap the loudspeakers were telling the crowds what he could not know: that Moss was out of his car and the mechanics were gazing hopelessly at the ruined engine. Ascari, already tired after 160 miles of difficult driving, was concentrating with every nerve. As he took the Casino Corner and wound the Lancia round the sinuous bends by the station he noticed that the spectators were waving and signalling to him. He had no way of knowing that they were trying to tell him that when he reached the pits he would be the leader. His deadly concentration on the task of taking the Lancia round the city circuit a little faster than seemed possible was broken. He sensed that something was wrong as he swung round the station bends and turned on to the Corniche road. He flashed into the tunnel and out into the brilliant sunlight to be confronted with the same gesticulations and excitement. It distracted his attention for a vital second as he covered the downhill approach to the Chicane and the corner became impossible. He chose the only way out and took the Lancia clean through the barriers into the sea. Concealed among the straw bales was an iron bollard the size of a small barrel. The car missed hitting it by about twelve inches.

It was a miraculous deliverance. Four days later, at Monza, Ascari was on his feet again, watching the practising for the Supercortemaggiore race. Just before going home to lunch with his wife he decided to try a few laps with the sports Ferrari of his friend Castellotti. In shirt sleeves, lounge suit trousers and a borrowed helmet he set off. As it emerged from a fast curve on the third lap the car unaccountably skidded, turned on its nose and somersaulted twice. Thrown out on the track Ascari suffered multiple injuries and died a few minutes later.

The strange element in our lives which we call coincidence played a disquieting part in the deaths of Antonio Ascari and his son Alberto.

Antonio was killed on July 26th, 1925, Alberto on May 26th, 1955. Both were aged 36 and at the height of their powers. Both had recently emerged from what seemed to be miraculous escapes. Both were killed because their cars skidded as they came away from a fast corner. In neither case was any explanation found for the disaster. Last of all both father and son regarded their racing helmets as their lucky charm. Both were killed the first time they ventured on the track wearing someone else's helmet.

Ascari's death was regarded as a national loss. Telegrams of sympathy were received from the heads of three foreign states. At his funeral Piazza del Duomo, the bustling centre of Milan, was packed with people. Normally the noisiest square in Italy it was that day so silent that the telephones could be heard ringing unanswered in the houses.

OFFICIAL RESULTS

1. Trintignant   Ferrari   2 hrs. 58 min. 9 8/10 secs.
                           105·9 k.p.h.=66·3 m.p.h.
2. Castellotti   Lancia   2 hrs. 58 min. 30 secs.
3. Perdisa   Maserati ⎫
4. Farina   Ferrari   ⎬ 99 laps
5. Villoresi   Lancia   ⎭
6. Chiron   Lancia   95 laps
7. Pollet   Gordini   91 laps
8. Taruffi/Frere Ferrari   86 laps

Fastest lap: Fangio 1 min. 42 secs. 4/10=110·568 k.p.h.

84

CHAPTER FOUR

THE WAY OF THE EXPERT

Belgian Grand Prix. Spa. 5 June

THE CARAVANSERAI of speed, which had split up temporarily to participate in sports car races in Italy, France and Germany, re-assembled at Spa ten days after the European Grand Prix.

Spa lies among the richly wooded Ardennes hills in the centre of a natural reserve. The medicinal qualities of its springs, known to the Romans as early as the first century, were not exploited by our present civilisation until the sixteenth century. However, Spa was still in time to be the first watering-place in Europe and the mother of all future spas. This quiet town claims notice on several other counts; it was the first place in Europe where games of chance were legally authorised, it staged the first horse-races ever to be held on the Continent and it saw the crowning of Miss Universe in 1932. A car race was organised in 1922 on the now famous circuit some five miles out of town.

The first Belgian Grand Prix, run in 1925, was also designated European Grand Prix. By one of those co-incidences which so often occur in the story of motor racing it was won by none other than Antonio Ascari, the father of Alberto. It was his last triumph, for it was in his next big race, the French Grand Prix, that he was killed.

The Belgian race was not run again till 1930 and then

85

it was won by that same Louis Chiron who finished sixth in the 1955 European Grand Prix at Monaco.

The three years before the war were dominated by the German cars, although a British driver all but joined the select company who have won this exacting race. Richard Seaman, the outstanding British driver of the pre-war era, piloted for Mercedes-Benz just as Moss does now. In 1939 he was leading the race when he crashed into the trees beside the road on the last bend before the final hairpin. Trapped in the wreckage when his car caught fire, he was burned to death. From that day the curve has been known as Seaman Corner.

Since the war the event has been held every year except 1948. The dominant figure has undoubtedly been Fangio. He was first in 1950 in an Alfa-Romeo. In 1951 in the same make of car, he was in the lead until forced to make a pit stop at half distance. A rear wheel jammed on the hub spline and delayed him for so long that he lost all chance of being placed. However, his reputation was enhanced by two feats: his new lap record of 120·51 m.p.h., which stood until he himself broke it in 1955, and the remarkable display of calmness and good temper which he had shown during that maddening pit stop. In 1954 he was victorious again and became one of the two men to have won the event twice. The other was Alberto Ascari, whose triumphs in the 1952 and '53 races revived the memory of his father's exploit twenty-seven years earlier.

The Spa-Francorchamps circuit consists of roads which are open to normal traffic all year and only closed for the three annual events held there: the motor cycle Grand Prix, the 24-hour Production Car Race and our particular Grand Prix. In the last twenty-five years various alterations have been made to smooth out some of the most acute corners. If you drive round it before race week it wears a most

86

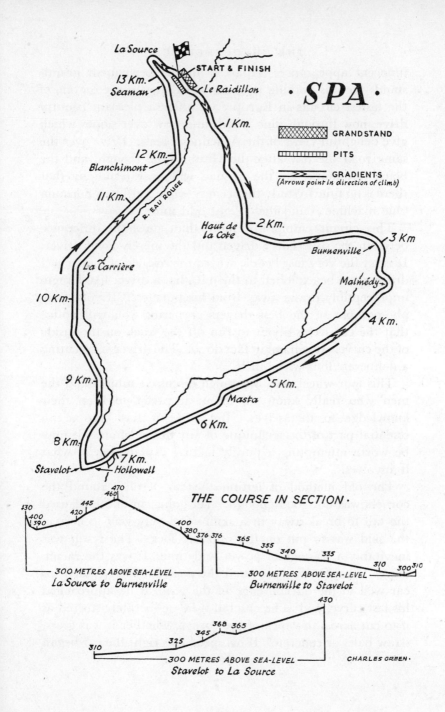

La Source

13 Km.
Seaman

START & FINISH

Le Raidillon

1 Km.

· SPA ·

▨ GRANDSTAND

▥ PITS

GRADIENTS
(Arrows point in direction of climb)

12 Km.
Blanchimont

11 Km.

R. EAU ROUGE

Haut de
la Cote

2 Km.

3 Km

Burnenville

Malmédy

La Carrière

10 Km.

4 Km.

9 Km.

5 Km.

Masta

6 Km.

8 Km.

7 Km.

Stavelot

Hollowell

THE COURSE IN SECTION ·

430
400
390

445
420

470
460

400
380 376 376

365
355 340

335

310
300 310

— 300 METRES ABOVE SEA-LEVEL —
La Source to Burnenville

— 300 METRES ABOVE SEA-LEVEL —
Burnenville to Stavelot

430

368 365
345
325

310

— 300 METRES ABOVE SEA-LEVEL —
Stavelot to La Source

CHARLES GREEN ·

innocent appearance. Apart from the permanent grand-stands there is nothing to show you that you are on one of the fastest circuits in Europe. It offers a pleasant country drive, now through pine woods and now over slopes which give delightful views of the Ardennes forests. Drive over the same road the day after the Grand Prix, though, and the black tyre-marks on the tarmac will bear testimony that there is no time to study the scenery while hurling a Formula One machine round these eight odd miles.

This circuit emphasises more than most the difference between the superlative driver and the merely good driver. It is on the very fast bends, where the science of four-wheel drifting can be exploited to the full, that a driver like Fangio imperceptibly draws away from his pursuers. If you study photographs of the best drivers cornering you will notice that the car seems about to run off the track on the inside of the curve. It will not in fact do so. The driver is executing a deliberate four-wheel drift.

This four-wheel drift is a much discussed subject and the men who really know all about it prefer to keep their knowledge to themselves. But since it has become an essential part of the technique of any driver of class it may be worth attempting a purely factual explanation of what it involves.

The old method of letting the car " roll " round the corners was not good enough. Yet going any faster caused the tail to break away in a skid. The only way to correct the skid was to put on the opposite lock. The result was inevitably a wastage of power and time. It was the racing driver himself who discovered the answer. He steadied his car well to the outside edge of the road as he approached his fast curve, and as he entered it he deliberately steered as if to cut across the apex of the corner, whether it was grass, straw bales or concrete. If his speed was right the car began to slide outwards under the pull of centrifugal force. The driver, with gravity and friction as his allies, used the power available through his rear wheels to counteract this pull and to push the car towards the apex of the corner and round it. It was unnecessary for him to steer in the ordinary way. Once the drift was initiated it was engine power that determined the car's course. All four wheels remained in perfect alignment, and the angle of drift depended on the frictional qualities of the road surface. Needless to say a very delicate balance of forces was needed. The sensation of the four-wheel drift has been compared to that of a skater who feels his feet going from under him. But if the driver loses his nerve and lifts his foot he will probably go off the road backwards on the outside of the curve.

The technicians began to scratch their heads. Heretofore it had always been assumed that slipping wheels offered less adhesion than rolling wheels. But in 1939 a certain Professor Eberan, an expert on racing car design, had stated that a certain degree of slipping increased the co-efficient of friction. Subsequent tests showed that the most effective results in braking and acceleration were obtained not with wheels still just " rolling " but when the degree of slip was 15 per cent.

What was true of tyre surfaces going in a straight line forwards was equally true of tyres slipping sideways. The racing driver was in fact instinctively inducing that 15 per cent of slip which gave him the maximum possible adhesion and enabled him to go round the corner several miles an hour faster.

Do not try it on an ordinary road with an ordinary car.

If four-wheel drifting is the stock in trade of the fastest driver, slip-streaming is a device which the man in a slower car often resorts to. It consists in allowing yourself to be pulled along in the air vortex behind the car in front. Any schoolboy who has tailed a lorry on his bike will understand about it. The ideal distance is about two lengths behind the leading car. This technique, if employed skilfully, has often enabled a car to keep up for lap after lap with a rival perhaps 20 m.p.h. faster. It was imported on to the Continent by British drivers who inevitably found their cars slower than the Italians. Apart from adding speed it saves petrol and reduces wear on the engine. But it is infuriating for the driver in front who will adopt severe methods to shake off the slip-streamer. He may do so by passing a third car at the very last moment before entering a corner and getting away on acceleration. If he is experienced and wily he may suddenly alter his line through a particular corner and take it very much faster. This will probably put the slip-streamer in difficulties and by the time he has sorted himself out the faster car is gone.

A good deal of psychological warfare takes place among the professional drivers. The old hand who finds a young hopeful obstinately clinging to his lead can soon unnerve him. As both of them slow for the curves he will bring the nose of his own car up till it is level with the other man's eye, now on his left side and now on his right. If that does not prove effective an even stronger hint can be given by a gentle shunt from directly behind.

But no driver of repute will go beyond a certain point. He knows the capabilities of his rivals and he will not deliberately do anything to cause them real danger.

These notes, written by Paul Frere, give some insight into the way a competitor must study the road he is going to race on. They are reprinted by permission of that most expert and artistic of racing periodicals, *Autocourse*.

" The non-skid tarmac surface is reasonably smooth throughout, except on the new fast Stavelot Bend, the foundations of which have settled down and made the surface bumpy.

" The start and finish line is just ahead of the pit area. Immediately after this comes *Virage de l'Eau Rouge* immediately followed by *Le Raidillon*. The two must be considered as one single left-right S-bend.

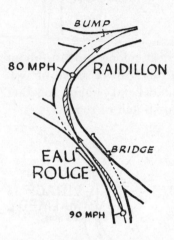

" Having passed the pits, the car must be taken as close as possible to the right-hand side of the road, then driven into the left-hand bend, drifting it as close as possible to the stone parapet of the bridge over the Eau Rouge. Coming out of the left-hander approximately in the middle of the road, the car is headed for the right-hand bend of the sharply rising hill. Being rather long and of irregular radius, this is a difficult bend to judge. The right-hand front wheel should be taken to the extreme verge of the road. Care should be taken not to let the car drift too wide when coming out of the corner, as there is a bad bump on the left-hand side, on the crest of the hill, over which a fast car will take off.

" Le Raidillon leads into the *Côte de Burnenville*, with a series of bends which cause no trouble, as they can be taken faster than the speed reached by present-day racing cars.

"At the top of the rise, there is a left-hand bend, usually called Virage du Haut de la Côte, which is tricky because it is blind and has a decreasing radius. Thus, the car should be taken on a rather wide line longer than the initial radius would suggest, letting it drift appreciably so that it is in alignment with the following straight, almost as soon as it can be seen.

" On the downhill stretch before Burnenville village comes a nameless bend, another left-hander which is blind but can be taken flat-out quite easily with a perfectly normal line cutting the bend at its apex.

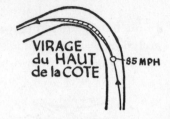

" Virage de Burnenville comes next, a long and fast (about 115 m.p.h.) corner, where much time can be saved or lost. This is made up of two right-hand bends linked together by a short approximately straight stretch of road.

" They should be taken as one single corner, letting the car drift rather wide out of the first part, then heading it for the right-hand kerb of the road, where it should be kept, in order to be correctly placed for the approach to the Virage de Malmédy. The left-hander, which can easily be entered as fast as the car will go, coming out of Virage de Burnenville, should be cut about the second telegraph pole, when it will be necessary to apply

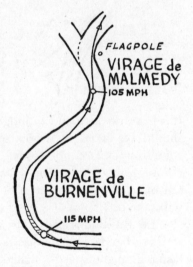

the brakes slightly for the right-hand Virage de Malmédy. This is a tricky one, because: (a) it is over a slight crest and cannot actually be seen at the precise moment when the car must be steered into it; (b) because the road is rather ad-versely cambered at that point. Fortunately, on race days, a flag pole is positioned on the inside of the corner, almost exactly opposite the point where it must be cut. It is essential that the car be headed for the corner rather early. If this is not done, the camber of the road makes the position difficult.

" The Virage de Masta, is a very fast left-right S-bend that can be taken at around 120 m.p.h. On the left-hander, the car should be taken close in, then aimed at the apex of the right-hander, which can be taken at full throttle once the speed has been adjusted for the first, left-hand part of the bend.

" From Virage de Masta, the straight proceeds, still downhill to Virage Hollowell and Virage de Stavelot, which are separated only by a short straight and should be taken as one single bend. Hollowell being slightly the faster of the two, the best way to deal with the section as a whole seems to be to cut Virage Hollowell rather before its apex, in order to come out wide early enough for the car to be correctly placed for Stavelot Bend. This is very bumpy and the best way to avoid the worst bumps is to take the car close inside the white line as soon as possible, and keep it there until the second bridge is passed, when the throttle may be

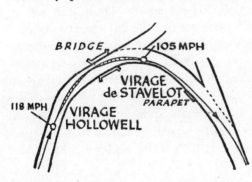

opened wide, allowing the car to drift gently out of the bend.

" The entrance to Virage de Stavelot is the lowest part of the circuit which, from there on, rises steadily back to

Francorchamps. Two left-hand bends which can easily be taken at the highest speed even by the fastest cars and a right-hander which, on a dry road, probably cannot be taken quite flat out by similar cars, lead to *Virage de la Carrière*. Although many a driver gets into trouble at this spot, it is really quite a straightforward 90 m.p.h. corner, which should be cut approximately at its apex, almost exactly where the telegraph pole stands. There is little margin left if the corner is misjudged, however, the ditch being very close to the outside of the road.

" Virage de Blanchimont, follows upon two more very fast bends, one easy right-hander and a left-hander which, being blind, is less easy. Blanchimont is a more acute, about 85 m.p.h. left-hand corner of which the apex is just hidden at the moment when the car must be steered into it. Prudence must be the keynote here, as there is practically no room left between the road and a precipice on the right.

" An easy right-hand bend comes next, followed by Virage Seaman, another fast bend of quite normal shape. Very little time is lost on this corner by playing safety first, as about 100 yards after the corner the car must be braked very hard indeed for Virage de la Source, with a maximum speed of about 30 m.p.h., in spite of good super-elevation. The corner is best taken in the normal manner, bearing in mind that the right-hand front wheel should be close to the inside of the corner just after its apex, so that the car can leave the corner accelerating hard. Thanks to the super-elevation, not much time is lost, if, by accident, the corner is taken a little wide.

" From here, the road leads back to the start and finish line."

Being the first Grande Epreuve since the death of Alberto Ascari, the Belgian Grand Prix was overshadowed by so recent a tragedy. The Lancia firm, deeming his loss irreparable, had announced that they were withdrawing definitely from racing.

Nevertheless, a small but interesting selection of cars and drivers had been accepted for the Belgian Grand Prix. A number of young men were ready and eager to dice with the Master—Fangio.

Fame did not come to Fangio easily or quickly. Perhaps that is why he carries it with such charm. Although he rose from a lowly station in life he seems to be a man who was born for greatness. He gives to his chosen art a dignity which enforces respect. Now that he has become famous he never shows impatience or discourtesy to the crowds whose admiration he has won. He will find time to sign the autograph books of a dozen small boys and to acknowledge with a wave the shouts of his supporters.

Juan Manuel Fangio, whose father was an Italian immigrant and a potato farmer, was born at Belcare, close to Buenos Aires, in September 1911. In fact, his birthday falls within ten days of Stirling Moss, though he is nearly twenty years older than his team-mate. A sportsman from his early days, he became in his spare time a first class footballer. But his first job was that of apprentice in a garage and he soon began to feel the attraction of fast machinery. Not till he was twenty-three was he able to scrape together enough money to hire a car and drive it in his first race. It was an old Ford and it broke down on him. But he was already infected with race fever. Soon afterwards he bought the first of a series of second-hand cars which he tuned himself and entered in races. He even constructed one to his own design. In between times he kept his hand in as a taxi-driver.

By 1948 he had achieved sufficient success in national races to have become a local celebrity. The Argentine Automobile Club, with Peron behind it, purchased for him

95

the latest model Maserati and were delighted to see him trounce the Italian drivers in the Mar del Plata Grand Prix. They sent him to Europe where he arrived on the scene like a bombshell. He won four races before his valiant Maserati wore out. His supporters bought him a Ferrari and with it he stepped straight into the top rank of drivers by winning The Monza Grand Prix itself.

Fangio had arrived. In recognition of the prestige he had won for his country, the Argentine Government presented him with £10,000.

The Alfa-Romeo team signed him up as their third driver for 1950, but Fangio was by temperament a number one driver. That year he won six Grands Prix and in 1951 took the title of World Champion. Resting on the laurels of these successes Alfa-Romeo decided to withdraw from racing. Finding himself at a loose end Fangio tried his hand at the B.R.M., but the British car repeatedly broke down under him. In 1953 he drove for the official Maserati team and his win at Monza put that firm back on the map again.

In 1954 when Mercedes-Benz returned to racing they made sure of securing the services of Fangio. Of the six Grands Prix which they entered he won four and never failed to bring his car to the finish.

If you met Fangio by chance you would never guess that he was the world's fastest driver. He is small, heavily built and walks with a rolling gait. His movements are slow and controlled. His eyes are remarkably calm and express a deep understanding of human nature. He talks quietly, without many gestures, and speaks Italian as well as Spanish. In repose his features have a sad though tranquil cast. Even when he is at the race-track he gives above all an impression of relaxation. Until he gets into the car he seems almost sleepy.

The moment his gear is engaged the whole tempo changes. Fangio is not only an artist but a fighter. You can see the former in the way he brings his car into the pit after a practice lap. The fighter appears during the struggle to decide who is going to lead the field into the first corner of a race. He is geared to win and if he can't win to bring his car to the finish. Half a dozen times he has brought a tired or battered car to the end by sheer courage and will-power.

He sits well back in the driving-seat, letting his body move easily to the movement of the car. His grip on the steering-wheel is low so that his arms appear to be relaxed. His face is unworried, almost slack. Often he chews meditatively as he drives. But his eyes are concentrated and intense, his gear changes almost brutal in their firmness. His driving is incisive and forceful and his reactions so swift that he is himself sometimes astonished at the results. He possesses all the natural gifts of the great driver and makes the whole performance look absurdly easy. He seems to require far less road space than anyone else and takes a far closer and tighter line on the corners. When driving the Mercedes he gives the impression that he is out for a pleasant jaunt in his car and could at any minute raise the lap speed by 5 m.p.h.

Wherever he races he is accompanied by his pretty and devoted wife, who takes a pride in waiting for him in his pit until he reaches the chequered flag.

When he decides to retire from racing, which he may well do at the end of this season, it will be to devote himself to his flourishing business in Buenos Aires. There he is the official Mercedes-Benz representative and owns a magnificent service station. As uncrowned king of the Argentine he will never lack customers.

For this 17th Belgian Grand Prix the field seemed to divide naturally into three groups:

THE OLDER SCHOOL :
- Dr. Giusseppe Farina (Italy)
- Juan Manuel Fangio (Argentine)
- Louis Rosier (France)
- Karl Kling (Germany)

YOUNGER MEN OF PROVEN ABILITY :
- Stirling Moss (Britain)
- Maurice Trintignant (France)
- Mike Hawthorn (Britain)
- Jean Behra (France)

YOUNG MEN WITH REPUTATIONS TO MAKE :
- Eugenio Castellotti (Italy)
- Paul Frere (Belgium)
- Luigi Musso (Italy)
- Roberto Mieres (Argentine)
- Cesare Perdisa (Italy)

Official teams had been entered by Mercedes, Ferrari and Maserati. Lancia had placed two cars at the disposal of Castellotti in deference to the young Italian's very special wishes. Castellotti had been Alberto Ascari's pupil and ardent admirer. It was he who had lent Ascari the car in which he had met his death. He had determined to win the Belgian race as a salute to the *Maestro*.

At 6.30 on the evening of the Thursday the throaty roar of the Mercedes-Benz W 197, echoing for the first time over the Ardennes hills, told the surrounding countryside that practising had begun. The air was so still that even from a neighbouring valley it was possible to follow the whole progress of the Mercedes' first exploratory lap by the rise and fall of the exhaust note.

During this first practice session no one was trying to record sensational times. Those who had raced at Spa

98

BELGIAN GRAND PRIX

ENTRY LIST

Driver				Car
Farina	..	..	..	.. Ferrari
Trintignant	..	..	.. Ferrari
Frere	..	..	..	.. Ferrari
Fangio	..	..	..	.. Mercedes
Kling	..	..	..	.. Mercedes
Moss	..	..	..	.. Mercedes
Behra	..	..	..	.. Maserati
Musso	..	..	..	.. Maserati
Mieres	..	..	..	.. Maserati
Perdisa	..	..	..	.. Maserati
Rosier	..	..	..	.. Maserati
Castellotti		..	..	.. Lancia
Claes	..	..	..	.. Maserati
Hawthorn ..	..	..	.. Vanwall

before were reviving their memories of the course. The newcomers, for instance Castellotti, were assessing the corners, studying the road surface, locating bumps which might deflect their car from its course at a crucial moment and choosing the landmarks which would indicate their cut-off points before corners. This was the time when the axle-ratios most suitable for the course would be selected and any other adjustments made to adapt the car to this particular circuit.

Friday evening was again sunny and conditions were ideal. The war of nerves had begun, but, more important than that, places on the front row of the starting grid were at stake. Fangio as usual was superb. He recorded a time of 4 minutes 18 6/10 seconds and said good-bye to the old record he had established four years earlier on a car with a much larger engine. Moss followed up with 4 minutes 19·2 seconds. Mercedes were pleased with this and brought their cars in. Meanwhile young Castellotti had been careering round and round and round on one or other of his two Lancias. Just before practice ended it was announced that he had done a lap in 4 minutes 8 1/10 seconds. This was the fastest speed ever recorded on the Francorchamps circuit and it had been achieved by a young driver seeing the course for the first time. Sensation! There was no time for the likes of Fangio to do anything about it now for practice was over.

Next day it rained and Castellotti's place of honour on the starting grid was assured. The course was almost awash with water and most drivers were content to splash round cautiously a few times to see what it was like. Three of the younger school showed their seriousness by going round again and again in the wet; Stirling Moss, Paul Frere and the inevitable Eugenio Castellotti. Watching him steaming round the long Stavelot curve at an almost suicidal speed one began to suspect that something more than the usual stakes were in this thing for Eugenio. Every time he passed he brought the memory of Ascari.

Race day dawned cloudy but dry. Spa is one of the most accessible of circuits being near at hand for French, Dutch, British and Germans. From break of day a vast international multitude was converging on the circuit. From Germany alone 18,000 cars were expected. The Germans needed no passport to come across the Belgian frontier and see the triumph of their machines. The two favourite viewpoints were the start where you command a unique view of $1\frac{1}{2}$ miles of road, and Stavelot where B.P. had set up about twenty TV screens disguised as petrol pumps. Watchers could thus obtain glimpses of the cars at several points on the course.

The last three hours before the start have always a special savour. There was no danger of the time between midday and three hanging on your hands. At first officialdom was dormant and everyone could enjoy themselves. Amateur photographers sneaked on to the track to take photos of the first cars to arrive. The road was closed soon to all cars but the competitors'. Drivers came swishing down in their private transport, stopped to unload kit at their pits, then took their cars round to the paddock at the back. Moss and Kling arrived in the saloons provided for their personal use by the Mercedes-Benz factory. Farina stood in the Ferrari pits, very thoughtful and withdrawn. Castellotti, making careful preparations, was much photographed and discovered that he had a number of dear friends whom he didn't know. From across the road the ladies commented on his long eyelashes and dark good looks. Hawthorn was dapper in white overall pants, bow tie and hacking jacket.

An hour before the start Royalty in the form of King

Leopold arrived. Scattered cries of "Vive le Roi!" from the somewhat puddingy Belgian crowd. A quiet and gentle-looking man in a blue Mercedes saloon came driving slowly down the road just at the moment when it was blocked by excited reporters and photographers. Beside him sat his dark, attractive wife. He gave a deferential toot and nosed his car politely round the edge of the crowd. It crawled towards the paddock entrance and turned in. Practically no one recognised him as the man who had burnt up almost every circuit in Europe and was about to win the Spa race for the third time.

There was just time for the drivers to be presented to the King before the cars were pushed to their positions on the starting grid. They had been allotted according to the best practice times and Castellotti was favourably placed for the first left-hand corner.

CASTELLOTTI		FANGIO			MOSS
Lancia		Mercedes			Mercedes
	FARINA			BEHRA	
	Ferrari			Maserati	
KLING		MUSSO			FRERE
Mercedes		Maserati			Ferrari
	HAWTHORN		TRINTIGNANT		
	Vanwall		Ferrari		
PERDISA		ROSIER			MIERES
Maserati		Maserati			Maserati

The start at Spa is cataclysmic. The road runs steeply downhill for three hundred yards before the left and right bend at Eau Rouge which leads on to a fast rising curve. This half-mile is like a section of a switchback. Just at the entry to the corner is the uncompromising end of the stone wall which flanks the road as it crosses the stream. The fact that it is painted white and black does not make it any softer.

Some of the teams had brought out the little batteries on wheels with the spline which they connect up to the front end of the crankshaft to start the car. Others, notably Maserati, were relying on the slope to help them push-start. The starter gathered the drivers round him and explained how he would set them moving.

The drivers dispersed to their cars. On the grass bank under the Royal Box three dark, plump men in yellow trousers and white shirts sat round a microphone. They were preparing to tell South America how Fangio won the Belgian Grand Prix.

Perhaps the presence of Castellotti in the pole position added to the drama of the last minute on the starting grid. Certainly the atmosphere of those moments is beyond description. The low cars with their silver, red, blue and green paintwork glittered wickedly in the sun. The drivers, already helmeted, inserted ear-plugs, fastened chin-straps and pulled on their gloves. With less than a minute to go the engines were started and the massed roar made one's thoughts reel. Just before he climbed into his car Fangio turned and saw the pale, set face of Castellotti. He stepped over, patted him on the shoulder and shouted a few friendly words. The drivers made haste to mount their machines and sat waiting with foot on the accelerator, gradually building revolutions up to two-thirds maximum. In the third row the mechanics were still frantically trying to push-start Musso's Maserati. People sitting with their legs dangling over the pit-counter thought better of it and tucked them out of the way.

Musso's car was taken to the back of the grid as the starting-flag was raised. The din became head-splitting. Castellotti began to nibble over the line. The flag fell and they were off. In the seconds before they reached the bend Fangio drew far enough ahead of Castellotti to take his water at Eau Rouge and lead him through the bend. On the rush up the steep slope Moss also passed him. Before the dozen cars disappeared into the woods almost a mile away the two Mercedes were distinctly ahead.

All the interest of this race was packed into the early stages. Four minutes later the sound of engines came from the hills across the valley. Spectators in the stands saw Fangio burst into view, followed closely by Moss. There was already a gap between them and Castellotti with nine other cars on his heels. As the leaders checked speed for the hairpin the whole field seemed to concertina up, but they opened out on the very rapid acceleration downhill past the pits. The pattern was familiar—Mercedes, Mercedes, Lancia; only this time it was not Ascari but Castellotti in pursuit. There was something very moving about this young man's determination to fill the gap left by Ascari. And he will. He may become the most brilliant driver of the decade.

The order at the end of lap 1 was: Fangio, Moss, Castellotti, Kling, Farina, Behra, Frere, Trintignant, Hawthorn, Musso, Mieres, Perdisa, Rosier. After three laps the German cars had established their superiority. Moss had almost the measure of Fangio but not quite. Castellotti, try as he might, just could not match them for speed on the fast curves. None the less he was the leader of a bunch of scrapping cars packed into a hundred yards of road—Farina, Kling, Behra, Frere.

The fourth lap brought more drama than the whole of the rest of the race put together. As Fangio came into view he was 6 seconds ahead of Moss. The distance between them lessened as they slowed. They seemed to take the hairpin almost together, but on the downhill run the gap stretched to a quarter of a mile. Behind came the same company, dangerously close together. Behra took the

Seaman curve too fast, gyrated wildly and shot off the road backwards, almost at the spot where Seaman was killed.

On the approach to the hairpin Farina decided to take some of the buck out of young Castellotti by passing him on the inside. Castellotti took him again on acceleration as they left the corner. Farina shook his fist. Castellotti replied by squeezing over so that Farina had to pass dangerously close to the pits. Just behind them the dog-fight between Kling and Musso had begun when the Italian shunted the German. Angry gestures were exchanged. Blood was warming up.

Meanwhile there was no sign of Behra. His car could be seen sticking its nose out of the ditch at an acute angle. It seemed impossible that he could have crashed at that speed and remained unhurt. Then a scarlet jersied figure appeared, trotting down the side of the road to the pits. Behra was received with joy into the arms of his thankful pit manager. Next time round Mierès was flagged in to hand over his car to Behra. The Frenchman set off again and within a few minutes of his narrow escape was driving for dear life round the circuit once more.

Fangio was putting on the pressure and the race average rose accordingly. Whereas Moss was on a string some 6 seconds behind, Castellotti's deficit had risen to 30 seconds and he was being threatened from behind by Farina. The third group consisted of Frere, Kling, and Musso, all with daggers drawn. These three were having a race far more exciting than anything going on up at the front. On lap 6 it was Frere who led. Passed by Kling in the course of the next lap he snapped ahead again as the Mercedes slowed for the hairpin. On lap 8 Musso had passed them both and Kling led Frere. They held that order for three laps and during that time the only British car retired from the race. Hawthorn had been lapping at about 4 minutes

40 seconds in eighth place. Now he brought the Vanwall in with an oil leak. So that was the sad end of another Grand Prix for the man who had defeated the Mercedes at Barcelona.

After ten laps Fangio began to catch up with the tailenders. Courteous signals were exchanged between him and old man Rosier as the silver car flashed past the blue. The crackle of Spanish from the grass bank under the Royal Box rose in volume. The Argentine commentator was giving his listeners full value. Fangio's average was worth wirelessing home about—193 k.p.h., or just about the round 120 m.p.h.

On the twelfth and thirteenth laps Castellotti was going just about as fast as the leader but on lap 14 Fangio set the new lap record with a time of 4 minutes 20·8 seconds. Two laps later came the news which robbed the race of its principal interest. Castellotti had come to a stop at Malmédy, his gearbox inoperative. So ended a fine effort. The crowd's sympathy for Castellotti was evident, but there were some who could not help feeling relieved that his bid with the lonely Lancia had not ended more dramatically.

Although Fangio's very fast drive was not overtaxing his motor the engines of certain competitors who were not going so quickly were being put to greater strain. Farina had closed up to a very steady third place. Kling had advanced to fourth behind him. It seemed likely that he would make a bid to range his Mercedes in line behind the others. But the younger school was in an uppish mood at Spa this year.

On the sixteenth lap Musso thrust his nose in front of Kling and came within 7 seconds of Farina. On lap 17 Kling led Musso: lap 18 Musso led Kling: lap 19 Kling led Musso. But the machinery was not relishing this duel as much as the men. On this lap, while Kling sped on through Eau Rouge and up the hill to the Burnenville

Forest, Musso coasted in to his pit. The mechanics got the car started again but the engine really was over-cooked. Only four laps later a trail of blue smoke followed Kling as he slowed for La Source. Tactfully he cut his engine and coasted in to the pits—to retire.

The Mercedes team had no desire to wash their dirty linen in public, but those who had seen the Mercedes debacle at Monaco noticed that the symptoms had been very similar. The question now was: would the same trouble strike at the two remaining Mercedes?

So now Frere, driving in his first Grand Prix for Ferrari, was a noble fourth before the eyes of his admiring compatriots. The announcer gave out the news that his average speed was higher than that of last year's winner. With 14 laps of the thirty-six still to run the race had become a procession—and a not very exciting one. The surviving eight cars were spread out over eight miles of circuit and there were long spaces when the spectators had nothing to watch. The purists were able to admire the perfection of Fangio's four-wheel drifts, and the surgeon-like precision with which Moss chose his line round La Source hairpin. But the drama-loving crowd had begun to drift away half an hour before the end.

In the open stand the crew of an Argentine ship, who had come all the way from Amsterdam to see the Champion race, unfurled their banner. It bore in huge blood-red letters the words:

FANGIO — MIERES
BUENA SUERTE

They moved down to the side of the track, hoping that their idol would see them and reward their pilgrimage with one wave of his illustrious hand.

Mercedes' team manager, Neubauer, appeared to be making efforts to slow his men down. Under the usual signal which had gone out on every single lap to tell the drivers their times appeared a new and mysterious board, bearing the letters R G. Neubauer even went so far as to kneel in the roadway as the Mercedes dashed past. British spectators, remembering the gremlin which takes a peculiar delight in knocking Moss out of races at the eleventh hour, anxiously watched for his re-appearance on each of those last half dozen laps. But the British driver was as steady as a rock, and when the two leaders set off for their final lap he was still just ten seconds away from Fangio, both of them travelling strictly in accordance with team instructions.

A minute and a half behind was Nino Farina. He had been World Champion in 1949 but now at the age of forty-eight was numbered among the veterans. Driving to fourth place and a rapturous welcome at the finishing-line went a driver whose career was only just beginning—Paul Frere.

A little over 4 minutes later Fangio crossed the line. He had won the race two years running and was the first man ever to win it three times. His fastest lap, having been made during the race, stood as a new record. His overall speed of 191·2 k.p.h. (118·84 m.p.h.), was the fastest at which the Belgian Grand Prix had ever been run.

Moss, who had been his shadow, was this time favoured with luck. His car had sprung an oil leak and during the last lap he was paddling in thick black liquid. As the car was pushed away into the paddock a rear tyre quietly subsided. One of the mechanics pulled from it a six-inch nail.

The jubilant Argentine ship's crew formed themselves into a line. On his lap of honour Fangio had seen them and sent them a wave and a smile. Their day was made. With their banner proudly carried aloft they bored their

way through the good-tempered crowd shouting: " Fangio!
Fangio! Fangio! Fangio! Fangio! "

OFFICIAL RESULTS

1. Fangio	Mercedes	2 hrs. 39 mins. 29 secs.
		191·2 k.p.h. = 118·84 m.p.h.
2. Moss	Mercedes	2 hrs. 39 mins. 37 secs.
3. Farina	Ferrari	2 hrs. 41 mins. 9·5 secs.
4. Frere	Ferrari	2 hrs. 42 mins. 54·5 secs.
5. Behra	Maserati	35 laps
6. Trintignant	Ferrari	35 laps
7. Musso	Maserati	34 laps
8. Perdisa	Mascrati	33 laps
9. Rosier	Maserati	33 laps

CHAPTER FIVE

THE END OF AN EPOCH

Les 24 heures du Mans. June 11-12

THE LE MANS 24-hour race was conceived in 1923 by
Georges Durand and Charles Faroux, the still active doyen
of French car racing. Their intention was to establish a
contest which would be a test bench for the kind of cars
used by ordinary people, as well as of their accessories and
the roads upon which they run. Thus the inevitable coming
of speed might be accompanied by a certain measure of
security. The annual contest at Le Mans has contributed
much to safety at speed. It is only fair to set against the
eighty-three lives lost in the 1955 disaster many unspecified
hundreds who would have perished in obscure car accidents
caused by inferior brakes, tyres, weight distribution or road
surfaces.

The Circuit Permanent de la Sarthe, to give the course
its proper title, lies 120 miles south-west of Paris on the
borders of the Château country. If you pass near there at
any time of the year you can take your own car round the
famous bends and see what speed you can achieve along
the fast Mulsanne straight. The grandstands and pits are
there all the year round, the length of the course is marked
out in prominent kilometre stones and placards with
diagrams of the corners will show you their shape before
you come to them. If your car is a very fast one and you
drive as rapidly as you dare you may get round in about

nine minutes. It will help you to appreciate what the new
lap record of 4 minutes 6·6 seconds means.

Since the 1920's when Sunbeams competed in Grands
Prix no big British manufacturer has entered the racing car
field. But Britain had ever been foremost in the design and
construction of sports cars. The lone Bentley driven by
Duff and Clement in the first race was the herald of a grand
army. The following year, again as a lone wolf, it achieved
the greatest distance. In 1927, '28, '29 and '30 the Bentley
team were gloriously victorious, and before the Second War
more British makes had inscribed their names in the records
—Aston-Martin, Riley, Lagonda, Alvis, Talbot, M.G.,
Singer. Since the race re-started in 1949 the British have
supplied a high proportion of the entries; the Jaguar works
team has three times brought home the winning car at
speeds previously undreamed of. Small wonder then that
enthusiasts in these islands have taken the 24-hour race to
their hearts and that thousands of them make it a point of
honour to be at Le Mans.

The significance of the race, however, is wider than this.
Le Mans is the most international event in the calendar.
Not only do cars from all the motor-manufacturing countries
compete, but the results are studied wherever cars are bought
and sold. So that with the vast increase in the sales of cars,
success under this unique spotlight is of incalculable value.
Not only will the manufacturer of the car placard his
success,[1] the name of every accessory in the victorious
machine will be shouted from the advertisements. Even
some fizzy drink may seek to boost its sales by telling the
world that the winning driver cannot live without it.

It has always been difficult for those who are not familiar
with this race to understand the results. A full explanation

[1]Jaguar, for whom the 1955 race was especially tragic, did not advertise
that year's victory.

risks being tedious. It can readily be appreciated, though, that if the organisers wished to attract cars of all types and sizes they would have to devise a system of handicapping. That is why the race had a double interest. Which car would most improve on the target speed set by the handicappers and win the Index of Performance, and which would cover the greatest distance and take the Grand Prix d'Endurance? Rarely did the same car accomplish both, and since sheer speed commands most respect the car which had gone farthest and fastest was regarded generally as The Winner.

It is not surprising that this race, which starts at four on a Saturday afternoon in June and goes on for all of a night and a day, has produced its full measure of comedy and tragedy. There is time for so much to happen; an often unbearable strain is put on machines continually stressed to the utmost and on men who cannot sleep. Up till 1955 there have been multiple crashes, miraculous escapes, but considering all things, remarkably few fatalities.

The first fatal crash, which occurred in the third year of the race, was quite inexplicable. No one was ever able to tell why Mestivier lost control of his Amilcar on a perfectly straight stretch of road. In 1927 there occurred the famous pile-up of cars at White House. S. C. H. Davis, the veteran writer and driver, approached the corner just as dusk was falling. He found the road completely blocked by the wreckage of five cars. His reflexes served him well, for though he walloped the crashed cars broadside on, he was able to take his battered Bentley on to victory eighteen and a half hours later. Then years afterwards at almost exactly the same spot six cars crashed in quick succession; the race had been on barely an hour. This time the results were tragic; René Kippeurt was killed instantly, and the British driver Pat Fairfield died during the night.

1951 was another sombre year. Only thirty minutes after the start the young French driver, Jacques Larivière misjudged, the Tertre Rouge corner and went over the protecting sand-bank into the garden below. He was killed outright and so it was never known why he approached this sharp corner at an impossible speed. In 1952 Pierre Levegh, in the Talbot which he had prepared at a cost of £10,000, attempted to drive single-handed for the 24 hours and win the race on his own. When he made his final refuelling stop three hours before the end he held an unassailable lead over the two pursuing Mercedes, but although he was so exhausted that he did not recognise his friends he refused to hand over or even to rest. Very soon afterwards the Talbot failed to come past, but this time the car was harmlessly at a stand-still between Arnage and White House. The crankshaft had broken. Many among the emotional French crowd were in tears as the exhausted driver was brought back to his pit and the way left open for a German victory.

In 1953 White House claimed another victim. During the tricky light of dawn, when mists rise along that low part of the course, the American driver Tom Cole brought his Ferrari through the treacherous bend too fast. The car somersaulted over and over and he was killed on the spot.

To lighten the picture as many and more miraculous escapes are recorded. At the finish of the very first race a certain Paul Gros was crossing the road to shake hands with someone he knew when a Chenard-Walker arrived at full speed. The car hit him and threw him twenty feet into the air; yet he lived to tell the tale. Maurice Post, the driver of a 1931 Bugatti, careered off the road at 100 m.p.h., and was unconscious for twenty minutes. He only lost his nerve when he was shown the wreckage of his car two months later, a spectacle which decided him to give up racing for good. In 1954 both Stewart and Bira crashed their Aston-

Martins and climbed virtually unscathed from cars that were no more than twisted horrors.

These are after all only the day to day hazards which drivers accept as part of their job.

Since the first Grand Prix d'Endurance was run thirty-two years ago this circuit has altered as much as the cars which race on it. Sections of it then were little more than narrow winding lanes and at one stage it dived through a suburban back street on the outskirts of Le Mans. Nowadays nearly all of the course is a wide smooth road. Only at one point does it narrow suddenly and alarmingly. There is no use in saying that it has been made safe, for the more the corners were opened out the faster the drivers went. But the banks which the organisers erected to protect the spectators were enough to stop a ten-ton lorry, and it seemed probable that a driver who crashed into them would only kill himself.

Le Mans is unique for the amenities it provides for competitors and spectators. During the war a combination of the German Air Force on the ground and the Allied Air Forces in the sky effected the destruction of the road and installations. By 1949 the zeal of the Automobile Club de l'Ouest had brought into being the magnificent new circuit of to-day. Six permanent grandstands face the long line of concrete compartments that form the pits. Behind the stands are restaurants, coffee and liquor bars, fruit, sweet and cigarette stalls. The area behind the pits, coyly named " Mon Village," consists of row upon row of display kiosks. There you can get everything from a new Peugeot to an early morning electric shave. In the " enceintes populaires," where many of the general public spend the entire 24 hours, circuses, music halls and shooting galleries are set up. You can even hear Mass said in the open air at 6.0, 9.0 and 11.0 on the Sunday morning. Beyond stretch the vast car-parks where thousands of vehicles have to be handled in such a way that their owners can find them and take them away whenever they want.

Through the middle of it all, coiling and grey like a black mamba, runs the roadway.

The competitor who takes his car out on to the circuit for the first trial laps may well feel that the course is straightforward and easy. He is a foolish man who does not listen carefully when a more experienced driver tells him how he should go round. Tony Rolt, the first man after the war to repeat the great Bentley triumphs, has recorded his opinion of the correct way to take the circuit. The first curve after the pits takes him in a wide sweep under the Dunlop footbridge and over a gentle rise to the Esse-bends one kilometre farther on. Changing down to second gear he gives a short burst of throttle to whip the tail into the correct position for each section of the corner. The second one requires special attention for it is sharper than the first. In rainy weather the road is slow to dry just here for it is flanked on either side by pine woods. Letting the car drift wide as he leaves the corner he has just time for a quick change up and down again before Tertre Rouge is upon him. Here the circuit joins the main Tours highway and the cambering of the road makes it essential to take the corner later than seems wise. Otherwise the lift of the tail over the hump will cause wheel-spin and the consequent slide may take him into the protecting sandbank. Ahead lie over four miles of very fast road where he may reach speeds of 180 m.p.h. At such velocities the slight kinks become bends that require the closest attention; if sudden gusts of wind burst through the gaps in the pine forest this two-minute surge of maximum speed will need skill and experience. It is on this section during the hours of darkness that the race is often lost and won.

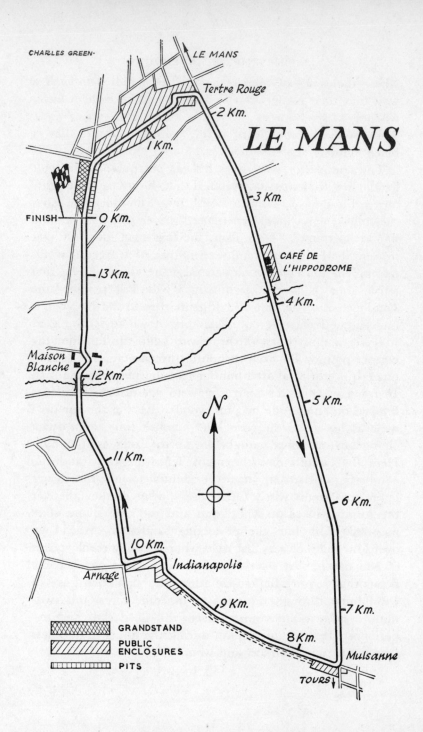

CHARLES GREEN·

LE MANS →

Tertre Rouge

2 Km.

1 Km.

LE MANS

3 Km.

FINISH — 0 Km.

CAFÉ DE
L'HIPPODROME

13 Km.

4 Km.

Maison
Blanche

12 Km.

N

5 Km.

11 Km.

6 Km.

10 Km.

Indianapolis

Arnage

9 Km.

7 Km.

8 Km.

GRANDSTAND
PUBLIC
ENCLOSURES
PITS

Mulsanne

TOURS ↓

The straight ends abruptly at the very sharp right-hand bend of Mulsanne. The corner is out of sight over the hump of a hill until it is only 400 metres away, so unless he wants to wear his brakes out he must be ready to start slowing the moment he sees it. Three changes down opposite the 300, 200 and 100 metre signs and he swings to the right in low gear. If his brakes should fail he can plunge on down the escape road leading to Tours, but if he tries to take his corner too fast he will end up in the sandbank; instead of saving seconds he will waste hours digging himself out. Taking care not to wag his tail on the treacherous surface he accelerates hard through the gears, goes through the first gentle bend flat out in third and floats over the next bending hill-top at something over 140 m.p.h.

Trouble ahead.

If he takes the right-hand corner before Indianapolis at 80 in third he can just scramble through the next one in second. In front of him some three hundred yards away is Arnage, where many a driver has spent fruitless hours shovelling sand. First gear and the same care as at Mulsanne are needed here. Now the pits are only three kilometres away, but the history of the race shows that they are the most dangerous on the course. Half-way between the eleven and twelve kilometre stones is a blind corner just over the brow of the hill. He must steer for it before he can see it yet keep his speed up to 120 m.p.h. White House itself can be taken at 115 m.p.h. in third gear if he chooses the right line. This corner has the worst name of them all. It is particularly hazardous in the early morning when inter- mittent mist drifts across to obscure it.

Now he can see the pits and grandstands ahead waiting like the narrow street of a village to engulf him. To the car travelling at 160 m.p.h. the kink just where the pits begin is a definite bend, and this is the very place where during the race he must take his eyes from the road to look for signals from his pit.

In the course of his lap he will have changed gear about twenty times. Without travelling at over 175 or under 30 m.p.h. he won't have broken any records, but he should have got round in about 4½ minutes.

At 9 o'clock on the Wednesday evening before the 1955 race 60 cars assembled at the pits for official practice. During the previous two days they had been scrutinised to make sure that they complied with the regulations. The visitor who had come expecting to see a production car race would have been forgiven for thinking that, like Rip Van Winkle, he had slept for twenty years, for no cars like these are seen on our roads to-day. This is because the race organisers, for reasons which to them no doubt seem good, have in recent years allowed manufacturers to enter proto-types of cars which they intend to build. The result is that beside cars which you can actually buy in a shop for £1,000, like the T.R.2 Triumph, are to be seen machines such as the Mercedes-Benz 300 S L R akin in most respects to a Grand Prix car.

Three makes which had already won the race since the war were represented by official teams—Mercedes-Benz, Ferrari and Jaguar. It seemed a foregone conclusion that one of them would win on distance.

A glance at the entry list (page 121) shows what a galaxy of racing stars had been engaged to drive these sports cars. Castellotti, Trintignant, Fangio, Moss, Schell, Mieres, Perdisa, Musso, Kling and Frere fresh from the Belgian and European Grands Prix; Maglioli, winner of the Carrera Panamericana; Rolt and Hamilton, winners of this race in 1953; Collins, Salvadori, Chapman, Parnell, victorious in countless British races; Hill, Fitch, Briggs-Cunningham from the United States; and for Jaguar the only Britisher, apart from Richard Seaman, to have ever won two Continental Grands Prix.

Michael Hawthorn was born in Yorkshire within six months of Stirling Moss, on April 10th, 1929, but he did not burst into the motor racing world until several years after his rival. Not many people got to hear of the driver who, during 1951, scored a number of successes in club events driving a pre-war Riley. Next year, 1952, he boarded one of the new Cooper-Bristols and tackled the most experienced drivers in their much faster cars. Handling his machine with great skill and daring he at once established himself as a man to watch. At Ulster he duelled with Taruffi, at Boreham with Villoresi. He finished third in the British Grand Prix and fourth in the European Grand Prix at Spa. Talent spotters from the Italian factories did not fail to point the moral, and 1953 saw Hawthorn with Ascari and Villoresi in the conquering Ferrari team. That year he won four important races, his final triumph being his five-yard victory over Fangio in the French Grand Prix. During this wheel to wheel battle which lasted 300 miles, even the spectators were fainting with excitement and, so intent was Hawthorn on winning, that he bit through his lower lip.

Still with Ferrari in 1954 he was badly burned at Syracuse when his car crashed and caught fire. Yet, despite this and the death of his father, he kept the flag flying and won a reputation for consistently finishing second. At a time when M.P.'s were crudely asking: " Why is this young man not doing his military service? " (Hawthorn was found unfit at the medical examination!) he came second in the British Grand Prix, Portuguese Grand Prix, European Grand Prix, the *Daily Telegraph* Trophy, the Ulster T.T., and the Italian Grand Prix. He clinched matters by winning the Spanish Grand Prix.

At the close of 1954 he was finding that his responsibilities to the family garage business at Farnham made it difficult to drive for foreign firms. He signed up to drive the British Vanwall in the Grands Prix and Jaguar in the sports car races of 1955.

He is tall, fair, very British-looking and tends to eccentricity in his track dress—a tweed cap with wavy brim, bow tie and hacking jacket on top of his racing overalls. He seems younger than his twenty-six years, especially just before or after a race. He does not belong to the armchair school of drivers. So far from relaxing, he leans forward with parted lips and seems to urge the car on. He is rather temperamental but on his day he can get a car round a circuit as fast as any man on earth.

Practising was scheduled to take place on three successive evenings—from 9.0 to midnight on Wednesday, from 7.0–11.0 on Thursday and from 9.0–11.0 on Friday. Even for this first session the race-conscious citizens of Le Mans had come bustling out to study the form. Never had the race been so open as this year and they knew that a titanic struggle was imminent. At one and sixpence a time they crowded the grandstands where a seat on race day would cost up to six pounds, or hurried to vantage points in the " enceintes populaires " where they could study technique on the corners.

Darkness was falling when the course was declared open, and the first cars pulled out for their exploratory laps. The roadway in front of the pits was a jumble of cars, mechanics, drivers, photographers and journalists. The Tower of Babel was a pious memory by comparison with this gabble.

In a very short time speeds began to rise. From the direction of White House pairs of headlights came peering up the road until with startling suddenness a car appeared

LE MANS GRAND PRIX D'ENDURANCE

Drivers	Car	Cubic Capacity
Parnell/Poore	Lagonda*	4,487
Rosier/Grignard	Talbot†	4,432
Maglioli/Hill	Ferrari*	4,412
Castellotti/Marzotto	Ferrari*	4,412
Trintignant/Schell	Ferrari*	4,412
Hawthorn/Bueb	Jaguar*	3,442
Rolt/Hamilton	Jaguar*	3,442
Beauman/Dewis	Jaguar*	3,442
Walters/Spear	Jaguar	3,442
Claes/Swaters	Jaguar	3,442
Whitehead/Whitehead	Cooper*	3,442
Helde/Lucas	Ferrari	3,000
Sparken/Gregory	Ferrari	3,000
Mieres/Perdisa	Maserati*	2,991
Valenzano/Musso	Maserati*	2,991
Manzon/Bayol	Gordini†	2,982
Fangio/Moss	Mercedes*	2,975
Levegh/Fitch	Mercedes*	2,975
Kling/Simon	Mercedes*	2,975
Cunningham/Johnson	Cunningham*	2,942
Collins/Frere	Aston-Martin*	2,922
Salvadori/Walker	Aston-Martin*	2,922
Brooks/Riseley-Prichard	Aston Martin	2,922
Macklin/Leston	Austin-Healey*	2,662
Colas/Dewez	Salmson	2,328
Dickson/Sanderson	Triumph*	1,991
Richardson/Haddley	Triumph*	1,991
Da Silva Ramos/Pollet	Gordini	1,987
Tomassi/Giardini	Maserati*	1,986
Wisdom/Fairman	Bristol*	1,979
Keen/Line	Bristol*	1,979
Wilson/Mayers	Bristol*	1,979

*entered by manufacturer. †entry withdrawn.

Drivers	Car	Cubic Capacity
Becquart/Stoop	Frazer-Nash*	1,977
Odlum/Vard	Frazer-Nash*	1,977
Polensky/Von Frankenberg	Porsche*	1,498
Riuggenberg/Gilomen	Porsche	1,498
Baxter/Deeley	Kieft*	1,493
Cabianca/Scorbati	Osca	1,491
Miles/Lockett	M.G.*	1,490
Jacobs/Flynn	M.G.*	1,490
McAlpine/Thomson	Connaught*	1,484
Russell/Taylor	Arnott†	1,097
Rippon/Merrick	Kieft*	1,097
Wadsworth/Brown	Cooper*	1,097
Chapman/Flockhart	Lotus*	1,097
Duntov/Veuillet	Porsche*	1,090
Chancel/Chancel	Panhard*	851
Cotton/Beaulieu	Panhard*	851
Hemard/Flahault	Panhard	747
Navarro/de Montremy	Panhard	747
Fayen/Rogenry	Moretti†	747
Ubezzi/Bellanger	Moretti†	747
Giraud-Cabantous/Lesur	V.P.*	747
Bonnet/Storez	D.B.*	745
Armagnac/Laureau	D.B.*	745
Héry/Trouis	D.B.	745
Faure/Duval	Stanguellini*	740
Damonte/Crovetto	Nardi*	735
Glockler/Juhan	Porsche*	1,498
Cornet/Mougin	D.B.*	745

RESERVES

Lund/Waeffler	M.G.	1,490
Olivier/Jeser	Porsche	1,498
Seidel/Gendebien	Porsche	1,398
L. Brooke/Morris/Goodall	Triumph	1,991
Savoye/Poch	Constantin	1,978

*entered by manufacturer. †entry withdrawn.

and slammed through the pit area. Watching drivers as they adjusted their goggles and accelerated away up the dark road, one could not escape a sense of foreboding. Seeing Le Mans for the first time by night you get the impression that the cars are going so very much faster than by day. With cars parked diagonally at their pits and even doubling up one outside the other as they stopped, the space left free for the fast cars to pass was desperately narrow. An eerie element was added by the spectacle of the new Mercedes air brake—a flap which rose mysteriously into an upright position behind the driver as he slowed for the Dunlop corner and sank out of sight as he disappeared from view.

However, the damage that evening was limited to one broken leg and one dented car. In the inevitable mix-up in front of the pits Moss's car and a D.B. Panhard had snapped at each other and the unfortunate Jean Behra was bashed against the pit-counter by the rebounding D.B. So his race ended before he had even time to practise.

Next evening during the hours of daylight everyone was ready to try seriously. Yet it was after dark that Mercedes-Benz cracked the old lap record of 4 minutes 16 8/10 seconds established by the winning Ferrari of Gonzalez in 1954. The new time of 4 minutes 15 1/10 seconds represented 119 m.p.h. That Mercedes could achieve this in the dark was enough to set everyone thinking deeply.

Just about this time the spectators in the grandstands came to their feet like one man. Taylor in the British Arnott had misjudged the bend after the tribunes and crashed. His car lay on the road, a hideous wreck. Instantly the yellow light across the road came on, winking its ominous warning to drivers coming up the straight. Fangio, approaching

very fast, did not seem to appreciate his danger. A girl
admirer of the World Champion shouted:

" Fangio, stop! "

The flap rose slowly behind the driver and he disappeared
into the corner on his usual line. All was well. The wrecked
car was on the inside of the long curve and its driver
had escaped unhurt. The yellow warning light was turned
off.

Jaguar were content to husband their cars for the race,
but it meant much to Ferrari to match the Mercedes lap
record on the last day of practice. There was an air of
gaiety in the Italian camp on the Friday evening. In the
area behind the pits the mechanics were rolling the spare
wheels down the slope like schoolboys playing with hoops.
It was all very much at variance with the German pit, where
a mechanic had been given the job of sawing the sharp
spikes off the pit railing lest someone in his excitement
should sit on them. On the Ferrari pit-counter Marzotto,
Maglioli and Castellotti stood waiting. They looked terribly
dépaysés in their check and corduroy caps, considered a *must*
for Italians at Le Mans. Castellotti was ready with helmet,
goggles and gloves as nine o'clock came up. He was hopping
in his eagerness to get out on the empty road while daylight
still lasted. The monster 4·4 litre Ferrari was the first
car to pull away when the course was declared open.
When Castellotti came past again he was going very
fast indeed. Stop-watches clicked in the Ferrari pit. The
next lap was a second worse than the Mercedes time
and Castellotti went by without even a glance at the pit.
On the following lap he went round the Sarthe circuit in
4 minutes 14 seconds and the chief mechanic flagged
him in. Darkness was falling and there seemed little
chance that anyone could now beat his time. Honour was
satisfied.

That evening's incident occurred just as people were packing up to go home. From the direction of White House a saloon car came hurrying up to the Gordini pit. Bayol had crashed at the notorious corner and was very badly injured. Silently the crowds watched the gate at the end of the pits open and the white ambulance creep out. With desperate slowness it moved along in front of the grandstands. Its square white shape disappeared under the Dunlop bridge. Bayol, gravely hurt, was lying only half a mile away, but it would have to go all the way round the circuit to reach him.

There was little more practising that evening. Long before the teams packed up and found their way back to the hotels the clock hands had moved past midnight and it was already Race Day.

*   *   *

If the following account of the 1955 race takes the form of a personal experience, I hope that anyone who happens to read it will not mind.

Nothing could be more gay than the Sarthe circuit on the morning of the race. The sun was shining brightly and the roofs of the cars already massing in the parks glittered and sparkled. The week-end of June 11-12-13 was Pentecost, the equivalent of our Whitsuntide. Flying machines trailing advertisements droned restfully across the sky and near the field where Wilbur Wright first got airborne from European soil, passenger planes were streaming in from all over the Continent. The flags of many nations fluttered their greens, reds, blues, yellows and white from above the pits, and all round the circuit a colourful, expectant crowd was converging on the best vantage points.

At midday the competing cars were lined up in front of their pits. There were still four hours to go, but much to be done. Tanks had to be drained under official eyes and refilled with the standard fuel supplied to every competitor. From a great tank back of the pits it came by pipe and flexible hose to the edge of the roadway. Team managers were supervising the packing of tools and spares. Only those carried on the car could be used if a break-down occurred. The police had not toughened up yet, and many people who did not possess one of the precious special passes were able to drift along in front of the cars, saying hallo to friends and inspecting the entries. The Jaguars, shaped like some deep sea monster with open mouth and tail fin, were shiniest of all. The huge $4\frac{1}{2}$ litre Ferraris looked fiery, red and angry. The tiny engine was completely lost somewhere inside the flat streamlined body of the D.B. Panhard. It seemed constructed especially so that an overtaking car could run straight over the top of it without noticing it. The Bristols with their single-seater bodies and stabilising fins resembled Grand Prix cars, but the Triumphs and the Austin-Healey might have been standing by the kerb of Kings' Parade in Cambridge. Many of the competition models built by small enthusiastic firms in Britain were represented. Perhaps the most interesting was the 1,100 c.c. Lotus with its Coventry Climax engine and disc brakes. Some of the practice times which Ron Flockhart had recorded in it had startled the Porsche brotherhood.

At 2.30 the filling of tanks with the approved fuel began. A formidable line of police filed out on to the track and prepared to go through the crowd as meticulously as a flea-comb. From now on only drivers and pit staff were allowed on the road. Even accredited photographers were hunted off by the gendarmerie, who had orders this year to be ruthless in applying the safety regulations. The official programme had warned spectators not to let papers fly on to the track, to fasten their dogs on a lead, to keep inside the proper enclosures. Otherwise consequences might be *un accident mortel—et un procès verbal par surcroît.*

The blue police jeep steamed up and down the road with shuddering aerial, while the high dignitaries of the gendarmerie drove about in an open Citroen, their stomachs exposed to the sunshine. Now and then the race directors would dash mysteriously round the course in the official car —a supernatural Bentley Continental. White cumulus clouds reared up on the horizon for a better look but decided to keep at a decent distance and let the sun go on shining over Le Mans.

At three o'clock the humming excitement mounted. A record crowd was already there. Even those who had numbered seats in the stands had taken their places. This last hour before the start was almost unbearable in its tension, further heightened by the first sound of the cars warming up their engines. The people round them now were not idle watchers, but overalled mechanics putting the finishing touches to months of work.

Thanks to the hospitality of the Le Mans Drivers' Club, I had for my own position a spot exactly at the start and finish line, opposite the timekeepers' stand. This was the point at the beginning of the pits area where the road kinks right. To the left I had a good view of all the pits and could keep an eye on the cars till they disappeared under the Dunlop bridge; to the right I could see down to White House. The road was about five feet in front of me, just on the other side of the waist-high protective bank. I had, in fact, chosen the exact spot at which the Mercedes was destined to crash.

The pre-ordained programme was being rigidly observed. At 3.20 the loudspeaker announced that it was time for competing cars to be brought to their starting positions. By

127

3.40 they were all lined up, the biggest at the front so that they could get clear away from the start, and the smallest at the rear. At the top end was the big Lagonda with beside it the Ferrari team; at the bottom the diminutive Nardi. This smallest car in the race was the most fantastic; it consisted of two torpedo-like tubes, one containing the engine and the other the driver. The Mercedes, although they promised to be the fastest cars in the race, were numbered 19, 20, 21, for their engines were only of 2·975 litres capacity.

Sixty cars in all were lined up at an angle along the road, for reserves had been called in to replace the non-starters. The Morettis arriving a couple of minutes after the stipulated time were disqualified and two more of the reserves were called in—another Triumph and Jacques Savoye's experimental Constantin. They represented France, Britain, the United States, Italy, Germany. One after the other the National Anthems were played, the music punctuated by the rasping of an engine being tested by a mechanic. The Italian flag was lowered to half-mast in honour of Alberto Ascari.

At 3.50 all engines had to be switched off. In the silence the sound of human voices became predominant.

It seemed impossible to believe that in ten minutes all these cars would be on their way. The drivers were fitting on their helmets and adjusting the straps of their goggles. On the road opposite each car is a little numbered circle in which the driver must be standing when the starter's flag falls.

The bearded pilot of the Nardi space-ship was grinding his teeth and studying the heavens. Bits of his engine were still on the roadway and the hands of the mechanic were trembling as he tried to put them together. There were only three minutes to go. A young woman came and laid

Le Mans. Cockpit of the Mercedes Benz 300 S L R. The mysterious knobs seen through the lower sector of the steering wheel are for squirting oil into any brake-drum showing a tendency to bind. The largest instrument is the tachometer marked in thousands of revolutions per minute   (*Photo Studio Wörner*)

Le Mans. One minute past four. The field attacks the " S " bends on the first lap   (*Photo Cahier*)

Le Mans. After one hour's racing the three leaders swing through the Esses—Castellotti (4) Hawthorn (6) Fangio (19) (*Photo Mailander*)

Le Mans. Castellotti has been disposed of and Jaguar leads Mercedes. Hawthorn and Fangio at Tertre Rouge shortly before they caught up with Levegh (*Photo Klemantaski*)

a hand on his shoulder and you could see his muscles relaxing.

Already the honorary starter was out on the road with his flag. This year it was Count Maggi of the Brescia Automobile Club. The great organisation that lies behind this race was all teed up and ready. Seven hundred police guarded the road to keep the foolhardy from risking their necks to gain a vantage point, 30 army signallers manned 25 telephone posts and 3 radio stations, 3 fire engines stood ready for a word from the Race Director's Headquarters midway along the pits. In 3 cottages temporarily leased as sick bays, 60 beds were available for the ailing or the injured. Twenty-five doctors stationed at the various first-aid posts around the circuit were ready to do anything from getting a fly out of your eye to delivering your baby. And in the famous Delagenière Clinic at Le Mans where doctors were still fighting for Bayol's life, special beds were held ready in case of injury to the drivers.

The loudspeaker voice was making matters worse by telling off the minutes. With only one to go the drivers seemed the calmest of all, though only they could know what was going on in their minds. To my left the people were standing on chairs to see better. The canvas of my folding stool had collapsed when I stood on it. I cursed it then, but a few hours later I blessed it. It was impossible to see the big cars at the head of the line from where I was, but I hoped to see something better—the pack as it came round at the end of the first lap.

A sudden scampering of feet up the road was the only sign that the flag had fallen. The drivers surged across the road in a wave, leapt into the driving-seat, started the engine. In a second the road was a mass of jockeying, weaving cars, fighting to gain an advantage before they disappeared under the Dunlop bridge. Even the little Nardi had gone, its engine buttoned together at the fifty-ninth minute. The road was left empty and the blue haze of exhaust smoke drifted up in the sunlight.

Already, nimble Castellotti had leapt into the lead. In what seemed only seconds the speaker gave us the order as they went round Tertre Rouge:

1.	Castellotti	Ferrari
2.	Maglioli	Ferrari
3.	Hawthorn	Jaguar
4.	Beauman	Jaguar

Through the trees came the sound of a mighty whirlwind going down the Mulsanne straight. One's imagination gave some idea of the hope, tension, striving and perhaps despair that was concentrated on those four miles of road. Nothing is like this first lap. Two minutes later we got the order from Mulsanne: Hawthorn had passed Maglioli and was second. We pictured them rocketing over the hill and down to Indianapolis. At Arnage the order was still the same. Everyone's eyes went to the distant spot where the ribbon of road came into view at White House.

A bare four minutes had gone by when the red car was suddenly there on the roadway. The pack was a good two hundred yards behind him as Castellotti came up the final stretch. So fast was he going that his car seemed to lift on its springs and settle again as he passed over the slight rise before the finishing line. Then he was past. In a wild blasting of sound the rest of the field went by; even after eight odd miles they were strung out over a third of the circuit. Before the last little 750 c.c. had popped past the pits Castellotti was already half-way down the Mulsanne straight again.

On lap 1 the order was:

1. Castellotti   Ferrari
2. Hawthorn   Jaguar
3. Maglioli   Ferrari
4. Walters   Jaguar
5. Beauman   Jaguar
6. Claes   Jaguar
7. Levegh   Mercedes
8. Salvadori   Aston-Martin
9. Parnell   Lagonda
10. Collins   Aston-Martin

Two favourites had not done well at the start. Fangio had not allowed himself to be panicked out of his relaxed calmness and had let the younger men do the scampering while he got under way with a steady heart and pulse. He was about half-way down the field while Rolt's Jaguar was right at the back among a gaggle of midgets. Both of them were slaughtering the smaller cars, Rolt screaming up the left-hand side of the road with his headlights blazing.

At the end of the second lap the first five cars were the same, but Fangio had performed prodigies and was already sixth, just in front of Levegh on the brother Mercedes. On that lap Castellotti broke the record with a time of 4 minutes 16 seconds, a speed of 117·9 m.p.h. Only three laps after the start the leading Ferrari was catching up the slowest cars. Fangio had come up to fourth place. What we had foreseen was now confirmed; Ferrari, Mercedes-Benz and Jaguar had each sent out one car with instructions to go full speed and break up the opposition. The drivers were the three stars of Grands Prix: Castellotti, Fangio, Hawthorn.

It was an effort to drag one's attention from the four

leaders and take an intelligent interest in what was happening elsewhere. The Cooper driven by the brothers Whitehead was very well up and in front of Kling's Mercedes. Trintignant, third man of the Ferrari team, was already in at his pit. The rear wheels were jacked up by one enthusiastic mechanic whilst another juggled with plugs. Trintignant, joint winner the year before, tried to remember that he still had a whole day in which to catch up.

At the end of lap 4 Hawthorn was right on Castellotti's tail with Fangio next but half a minute behind. During the next tour the World Champion established a rew record at 119 m.p.h., and crept even closer. Cars were continually passing now, little ones all mixed up with big ones. But the slower machines were righteously keeping in mind an instruction issued by Charles Faroux as far back as 1950. " In passing the grandstands the small cars must never encroach on the left-hand side of the road which is divided by a white line. I stress this because it is of the greatest importance." The long crocodile of police which had curtained off the pit area formed itself and marched away to jokes and *vin rouge* behind the pits. Enough stalwarts were left to shoo away those who were foolish enough to climb the wattle fences and perch on the safety bank.

The loudspeaker system, with what seemed unpardonable indifference, took time off for a few snatches of music and a couple of irrelevant announcements. It seemed indecent to speak of anything but the amazing race going on before our eyes. Fangio took the record with a new speed of 120 m.p.h., with a time of 4 minutes 13 seconds. Both he and Hawthorn were closing on Castellotti. The Jaguar was only 4 seconds behind the Ferrari.

Fangio was making one of those attacks which have

brought him the World Championship. On eight miles of road packed with sixty cars he lowered the lap record to 4 minutes 10 seconds, and at the end of the twelfth lap passed Hawthorn bang in front of the grandstands.

The gauntlet was down.

On the thirteenth lap, after one hour's racing, the three leading cars streamed up the final straight and past the pits with only 5 seconds dividing them. Hawthorn was in front of Fangio again. The rest of the field was out-distanced.

1.	Castellotti	Ferrari
2.	Hawthorn	Jaguar
3.	Fangio	Mercedes-Benz
4.	Maglioli	Ferrari
5.	Walters	Jaguar
6.	Kling	Mercedes-Benz
7.	Levegh	Mercedes-Benz
8.	Beauman	Jaguar
9.	Rolt	Jaguar
10.	Mieres	Maserati

Collins, Aston-Martin, was on the same lap as the leader but had dropped to 15th. He was driving steadily and at a sensible pace. Rolt by that time had passed one car for almost every minute of the race.

No one was asking for his money back now. A great race had been promised, and this was a race to tell your grand-children about. People in the rear looked for boxes, empty tins—anything they could stand on for a better view. The pit-counters were still crammed with men and women, and every four minutes thousands of eyes focused on the road down by White House to see who would appear first.

Away on the far side of the circuit at the end of the long straight, Hawthorn brought his Jaguar up alongside the

133

Ferrari and beat it into the corner. His lead was only momentary. Before they reached the grandstands Castellotti was in front again; Fangio and Hawthorn were wheel to wheel and neither wanted to give way as they charged the Dunlop bridge. On that next lap they both passed the Ferrari.

Castellotti had had his hour. He was with them next time round, but from then on he was left farther and farther behind. The Ferrari's overtaxed engine was not able to cope with the ever-mounting speed.

The next hour saw one of the greatest duels in motor racing history, and one of the most thrilling spectacles ever offered to a crowd of 300,000. Under the blue sky and faithful sun, colour, speed and daring combined to bring the lustre of a bygone age to modern motor-racing. Hawthorn is a real racer, one of the first five. He had raced Fangio before and beaten him, but on a foreign car. His efforts during the 1955 Grands Prix season to drive a British car to success had been frustrated by mechanical failure. Now he could match Fangio in a British car and his instructions to drive fast suited his temperament.

On the eighteenth lap Fangio caught Hawthorn in the narrow channel of road between pit and stands. Hearts stopped beating as the Argentine surged past into the lead at the very moment when both cars were taking the curve under the Dunlop bridge. It was a momentary advantage. Hawthorn got in front again on the Mulsanne straight.

The record became a coconut-shy. On the twentieth lap Fangio knocked it down with 4 minutes 8 8/10 seconds and took the lead; on the twenty-second he lowered it to 4 minutes 8 seconds. After two hours' racing the Mercedes was out in front. It seemed that Fangio's attack had prevailed. But Hawthorn would not have it so. With a scorching lap at 122·4 m.p.h., he established the record at 4 minutes 6·6 seconds and took a 4 seconds' advantage over Fangio. Castellotti had been left 30 seconds in arrears; as he passed his pit he thumped the side of his car with one hand. The face of Ferrari's chief mechanic, Meazza, registered his bewilderment at this signal.

For the start of a 24-hour endurance contest this high-speed duel was fantastic. The men making cool-headed calculations in the Ferrari–Jaguar–Mercedes pits countenanced it because each was confident that their car would be the only one to stand the pace. For Fangio and Hawthorn the issue was a simple one: they were racing.

At the end of the second hour this was the order:

1.	Fangio	Mercedes
2.	Hawthorn	Jaguar
3.	Castellotti	Ferrari
4.	Maglioli	Ferrari
5.	Kling	Mercedes
6.	Levegh	Mercedes
7.	Walters	Jaguar
8.	Rolt	Jaguar
9.	Beauman	Jaguar
10.	Musso	Maserati

Rolt at this point was travelling faster than anyone except the two leaders. His times on the thirty-first, thirty-second and thirty-third laps were 4 minutes 12·3 seconds, 4 minutes 12·8 seconds, 4 minutes 12·6 seconds—a model of consistency at speed.

During the next few laps the lead was changing constantly. Sometimes as they raced up the road towards the stands they were neck and neck. Fangio's speed on the Mulsanne straight was 181·5 m.p.h., but Hawthorn was able to take his Jaguar faster through the bends.

At 6.15, Castellotti was 1 minute 15 seconds behind the leaders, Maglioli 3 minutes 20 seconds, and the second and third Mercedes driven by Kling and Levegh 3 minutes 45 seconds behind. These last two were lapping steadily in team order only fifty yards apart. But Fangio and Hawthorn were only half a minute behind them on the road. Within the next few laps they would have to think about passing cars travelling almost as fast as themselves. Another factor was arising; pit calculations showed that fuel was running low and signals had been made from the Jaguar, Mercedes and Ferrari pits. How these drivers could be expected to spot them as they tore through the narrow pit area passed the comprehension of ordinary mortals.

Unaware that the cards were stacked for disaster the announcer broke off his commentary for two announcements.

The condition of Bayol was critical. And would the parents of little Marie Dupont, aged three, please come and claim her at the steps under the Press stand?

On lap 34 Fangio and Hawthorn passed almost level— as usual. Meazza was out on the road in front of the Ferrari pit. We saw Castellotti braking hard as he swung over to the right of the road. He stopped accurately opposite his pit with all four wheels locked, cut off the engine and jumped on to the pit-counter to brief Marzotto, his second driver.

Stop-watches had clicked. It was obvious that all that had been gained by two hours' furious driving could be lost by an inefficient pit stop. The Ferrari mechanics bundled fuel into the tank, snapped the filter cap down. Marzotto jumped straight from the counter into the driving-seat, started the engine and was away. The Ferrari had been stationary $1\frac{1}{2}$ minutes.

Fangio and Hawthorn were only 60 seconds away.

Statements issued later gave some idea of what had happened during that all-important lap. Hawthorn knew that he would stop at his pit next time he passed. He had already been given the " come in " signal twice. The Jaguar pit system requires drivers to complete two more laps after receiving the signal, and to come in at the start of the third. The wisdom of such a rule was borne out by events, although it was interpreted to the disadvantage of Hawthorn who was accused of ignoring pit signals. During his thirty-fifth lap he managed to stretch the distance between himself and Fangio to nearly 8 seconds. At Arnage he caught and passed Levegh. Coming up the straight from White House he caught and passed Macklin's Austin-Healey —a car of the same engine capacity and also fitted with disc brakes.

Ahead in the pit area Meazza's flag had flashed to call Maglioli in and the Jaguar pit staff were all set to refuel the leading Jaguar. The Mercedes pit were preparing to receive Kling, at that moment somewhere down near White House.

Realising that the leaders were due in a few seconds, I looked down towards White House and said to myself: " Here they come! " The road seemed to be congested with cars. Hawthorn was well over to the right and already slowing some 250 yards before the beginning of the pit area. It was perfectly obvious that he was making a premeditated pit stop and equally obvious that he did not intend to waste any time over it. A green car later identified as Macklin's was there too, but my chief impression was of a silver car coming up at enormous speed. I took it for Fangio, but in fact it was Levegh. The Mercedes did not seem to be using all the space available on the left of the road, possibly because its driver knew that he had a slight bend to deal with in 200 yards. When the Austin-Healey pulled out to pass the Jaguar the three cars were not so much abreast as in echelon—Jaguar, Austin-Healey and Mercedes-Benz.

I doubt if the first part of the accident was recorded by any camera. The Mercedes touched the Austin Healey (other accounts indicate that the Mercedes' right front-wheel touched the Austin-Healey's left rear). During the ensuing 1/5 second (at an approximate velocity of 200 feet per second) the Mercedes, instead of steering to follow the changing line of the road, glanced slightly to the left and headed for the safety bank. It was still on the road when it hit the bank about ten feet to my right. Instead of becoming embedded in the safety wall the left front wheel rode up it and the car leapt. The next instant was curiously drawn out, like a film suddenly in slow motion. I could see the under part of the Mercedes as it passed over my head, still in one piece and identifiable as a car with driver aboard. It seemed to fly on as leisurely as the horses going over Becher's Brook in the newsreel.

Though I did not realise it at the time it snapped a wire at a point eighteen inches above my head and sprinkled the hair of the lady on my right with tiny morsels of silver coachwork.

Even while the silver car was still hurtling to earth again there was time to feel emotion. First came anguish for the driver, imprisoned in that airborne car, utterly committed to the crash. Then came the sensation of violation, of tremendous forces suddenly out of control. Last and most terrible was the realisation that the machine was falling amongst a mass of humans and must surely crush them.

While another part of my mind registered the whirling Austin-Healey on the roadway and a third unidentified car somehow mixed up in it all, I saw the Mercedes bounce, some thirty yards from its first point of take-off. The crushing sound of its landing is unforgettable.

That was its first contact with the earth and it was this shock which I believe to have caused its disintegration. This was the point at which the photo-sequences I have seen began. They show how the engine and parts of the chassis were catapulted on through the crowd. From where I stood I saw the carcase of the car bounce and land again some fifty yards away and with a final merciful twist, heave itself out of the crowd up on to the safety wall.

There followed a moment of utter silence and shock. The thing had happened but no mind could yet measure its extent. From the wreck a few red flames sprouted. The gyrating car had gone on out of sight and the third machine was not to be seen. I felt they must surely have been destroyed.

The instant of stillness was broken even as the first gendarmes leapt across the road to the rescue. The Mercedes exploded with a whump into white flame, and I became aware of the scene to my immediate left.

Those who had been standing on chairs were now prone. The little enclosure was a jumble of broken chairs and un-moving forms. Here there were no wounded. All were dead, many decapitated. Those who were still living had recoiled from the dead in a movement of instinctive and superstitious dread.

There followed scenes which are an inevitable part of human experience. One must face them and accept their implications for they are a portion of truth. But it is better not to write about them.

All of us who were near felt curiously identified with the people who had died. We too had felt the shock, like the branches of a tree that trembles at the woodcutter's stroke.

There have been disasters before. Why did the Le Mans

disaster seem so cruel, so shocking? I think it was because the source of so much pleasure and glamour had suddenly become the cause of tragedy beyond imagination. There is no adequate simile, but it was in a way as if a trusted pet had become a mad dog among children at play.

As for the causes, much has been written and said about them by some who have thought and many who have not.

Mercedes-Benz issued a long statement very soon after the event. Jaguar followed it with another briefer one. Both firms intended to show that their drivers were not to blame. Macklin, as a private owner, had no one to speak for him. Having studied both the other reports I asked him whether he would like to give his views. His answer, after much thought, was that he preferred not to comment, since what he said might inadvertently seem to put the blame on someone else. He pointed out that the inquiring body would duly issue its findings as it thought fit. However, since many months have passed and no statement has been made by the F.I.A., it seems reasonable that this book should attempt to present the facts as they appeared to an impartial observer.

At the start it is worth emphasising two important points. Firstly, that all the drivers involved were of proven ability. Secondly, that the cars were of approximately the same engine size.

A study of the road where the accident occurred will do much to explain it. At the precise spot where the Mercedes hit the bank the road kinks to the right. For the fastest cars this is a definite bend, and every car driver knows that it is not possible to hug the outside edge of a fast corner. If a car is travelling slowly in order to stop at its pit it has the same effect, as it passes the kink in the road, as a car parked on the bend. So that although the measurable width of the road is constant the effective width may be drastically reduced. Travelling for various reasons at various speeds three cars reached this point simultaneously. Hawthorn, slowing for his pit, occupied the inside station on the corner. Macklin steered out to pass him. Levegh, moving very fast, was already committed to a certain line as he aimed his car for the corner. In attempting to squeeze past Macklin, he touched wheels with him. While the Austin-Healey spun wildly, the Mercedes was deflected towards the bank and within a split second was airborne.

How it rode up the bank and travelled through the air in one piece is a mystery. Not much earth was displaced and my own view is that only the left front wheel collided substantially with the bank. The car rose, spinning, and only disintegrated when it landed again for the first time twenty to thirty yards farther on.

Hundreds of witnesses have given their accounts of these three seconds. But the one vital testimony must for ever be lacking—that of Pierre Levegh.

While priests moved among the dying and the medical services swung into action a column of smoke rose from the direction of White House. Jacob's M.G. had turned over and caught fire. The driver was seriously injured. Other drivers, unaware of so great a disaster, slowed down to pass through the smoke that billowed across the road at two points and then drove on.

Fangio had been following several hundred yards behind Levegh. He had seen the Frenchman's signal that he was about to pass another car and slackened speed. When the crash occurred he was able to slip past the spinning Austin-Healey, only dimly aware of the somersaulting car to his left.

Hawthorn, slowing at his pit, had seen it all. With one car thrashing among the spectators and another skidding madly all over the road, is it any great wonder that he overshot his pit? Yet Mercedes saw in this a sign that he

had been going too fast to stop and said so afterwards in a
statement to the press. There was great talk in the popular
French and Italian press about Hawthorn's unpremeditated
braking. It was all nonsense. But shocked by what he had
seen he completed another lap and handed over to his
second driver, Ivor Bueb.

Fangio completed his lap and came to his pit. Smoke
was pouring across the road and the scenes beyond the
palings were heartbreaking. It was in these conditions that
Stirling Moss was presented with the number one Mercedes.
He jumped in and continued the drive.

The race was going on.

Charles Faroux was faced with a decision that was not
easy. It took more courage to let the race go on than to
stop it. By his steadiness and inflexibility he averted the
general stampede which would have made impossible the
work of rescue, the summoning of friends and relatives, the
effective employment of doctors and communications. There
were well over a quarter of a million people round that race
track. Secondly, the continuation of the race was an
affirmation that what had happened was an accident due
to a combination of circumstances which might not repeat
themselves for another thirty years. But it placed a terrible
responsibility upon the drivers.

More than ever before the race had become a test of
endurance for drivers, organisers and spectators.

For some time my thoughts and attentions were elsewhere
and it was not till two hours later that I managed to get
some grip on the progress of the race. A study of the official
lap times show how the disaster had affected the outcome.
The leading Jaguar had been lapping at around 4 minutes
10 seconds. For the thirty-sixth and thirty-seventh laps its
times were 6 minutes 31 seconds and 6 minutes 37·6 seconds.
The leading Mercedes continued at slightly diminished

speed until lap 41, when the time of 6 minutes 21·7 seconds indicates where Fangio handed over to Moss. Perhaps the most remarkable lap in the whole race was Moss's fifty-third, accomplished in 4 minutes 8 seconds. Gallantly though Bueb tried, he could only record 4 minutes 51·5 seconds on the same lap. By eight o'clock the British car was almost two laps behind the German. Castellotti had vanished from the scene; his Ferrari was in the dead car park with a split cylinder block.

After four hours of racing the first ten cars were well spaced out:

1. Fangio/Moss	Mercedes	55	laps
2. Hawthorn/Bueb	Jaguar	54	,,
3. Maglioli/Hill	Ferrari	54	,,
4. Rolt/Hamilton	Jaguar	54	,,
5. Beauman/Dewis	Jaguar	53	,,
6. Musso Valenzano	Maserati	53	,,
7. Castellotti/Marzotto	Ferrari	52	,,
8. Parnell/Poore	Lagonda	52	,,
9. Claes/Swaters	Jaguar	52	,,
10. Kling/Simon	Mercedes	52	,,

Car number 37, the 1½ litre Porsche, which was destined to finish in fourth position among cars with twice its engine size, was at this point eighteenth with 48 laps to its credit.

By 9.30 all the competing cars had switched their lights on. With the fall of darkness a terrible gloom settled on the scene. An announcement gave the death roll as fifty odd. When the voice was switched off there was silence, instead of the gay music so typical of Le Mans. The blaring exhaust-notes of the cars as they went by echoed from the pits and the half-empty stands. The inquisitive had come to gaze at the enclosure where so many people had died. Gradually the fatal spot filled up again with spectators.

By ten o'clock a whole age of racing seemed to have passed, but this was only quarter distance.

1. Fangio/Moss	Mercedes	83	laps
2. Hawthorn/Bueb	Jaguar	81	,,
3. Rolt/Hamilton	Jaguar	80	,,
4. Beauman/Dewis	Jaguar	79	,,
5. Kling/Simon	Mercedes	79	,,
6. Valenzano/Musso	Maserati	78	,,
7. Collins/Frere	Aston-Martin	78	,,
8. Swaters/Claes	Jaguar	78	,,
9. Parnell/Poore	Lagonda	77	,,
10. Maglioli/Hill	Ferrari	76	,,

Taking the handicapping system into account the same three cars were in the first positions, but after them there was some variation. For once the biggest cars were doing best in the *Classement à l'indice*.[1]

		Index figures of performance
1. Fangio/Moss	Mercedes	1·359
2. Hawthorn/Bueb	Jaguar	1·313
3. Rolt/Hamilton	Jaguar	1·297
4. Kling/Simon	Mercedes	1·289
5. Maglioli/Hill	Ferrari	1·285
6. Beauman/Dewis	Jaguar	1·285
7. Russo/Valenzano	Maserati	1·279
8. Collins/Frere	Aston-Martin	1.277
9. Polensky/Frankenberg	Porsche	1·276
10. Glockler/Juhan	Porsche	1·273

The fortunes of Ferrari had sadly declined, but Jaguar were in a very strong position. A most interesting develop-

[1] The handicappers had decreed a target speed for each car based on its engine capacity. The Index of Performance showed at any stage of the race to what extent a car was improving on its target figure or otherwise. Put in other words, the Mercedes was travelling 1·359 times faster than anticipated.

Le Mans. An instant after the crash. a. Hawthorn slowing. b. Fangio weaving through. c. Point where the Mercedes first struck the bank. d. Macklin in the throes of the spin which will bring him to the toes of the photographer and finish out of the picture. e. The Mercedes hulk falling amongst people after its second bounce. f. & g. A wheel, the rear axle assembly and the engine were projected further. This photo (*copyright* "*Match*") is from the French television film

Le Mans. This picture was taken from the spot where the Mercedes driven by Levegh had leapt the safety bank a few seconds before   (*Photo Rutherford*)

Le Mans. A Jaguar makes a midnight pit stop to refuel, change tyres and swap drivers (*Photo Klemantaski*)

Le Mans. Gloomy Sunday. Dawn breaks over White House, as Collins' Aston-Martin overhauls Duntov's Porsche. The Salmson lies abandoned in the ditch (*Photo Klemantaski*)

ment was the appearance of the Aston-Martin in seventh position.

As the evening wore on the loudspeaker read out the long lists of relatives whose presence was urgently requested at Le Mans. By midnight the death-roll was known to have risen to sixty. There was a nightmare quality in the sound of the Mercedes and Jaguar drumming relentlessly round the eight miles of dark road. A minute after the twin tail lights had disappeared under the Dunlop bridge you could hear the distant note of the exhaust as the car accelerated away from Tertre Rouge for the mad career down Mulsanne straight.

The announcer's voice was lugubrious as he read out the order at midnight. Forty-six cars were still running out of the original sixty.

A walk up through the public enclosures to Tertre Rouge revealed strange sights; an old woman huddled against a tree with her chin on her knees, a small boy stretched out asleep beside his suitcase. You had to be careful lest in the darkness you stepped on a sleeping form. A few yards away the cars were squirting through the Esses, their headlights swinging long beams through the pine trees. Here there was some attempt at gaiety; the beer halls and bars were open, the side shows and roundabouts raking in as many customers as they could.

The hours of darkness represent one-third of the race and while many of the spectators are away snatching a few hours' sleep some of the most significant events take place. Soon after midnight Jaguar number 8, driven by Beauman, skidded into the sandbank at Arnage and for a couple of hours the driver vainly worked to dig it out. The little Lotus, lapping at up to 95 m.p.h., gained twelve places between the hours of 10 p.m. and 1 a.m., only to be disqualified on a technical offence. At 2.0 a.m. those who were awake tried to analyse a subtle change that had occurred in the texture of sound. The harsh angry note of the Mercedes, so reminiscent of the Grand Prix car, was silenced. A few minutes later we knew the reason. After long delays caused by the congestion of the telephone wires the Mercedes team had made contact with their directors at Stuttgart. The decision was taken to withdraw the remaining cars as a sign of mourning. Long before dawn creaked open the entire Mercedes caravanserai had gone, leaving an empty square space behind the pits allotted to them. The record-breaking Jaguar was left in the lead.

The race now lacked its principal interest. The order at the time of the withdrawal was Mercedes—Jaguar—Jaguar —Mercedes with the Aston-Martin holding a watching brief farther back. The end of the race might well have seen a renewal of the duel with which it had started and the Jaguar, which had proved itself the fastest car in the race, could have scored a more worthwhile victory.

4.0 a.m. was a miserable hour to reach half-distance, but in normal times the order on distance would have brought pleasure to British spectators.

1.	Hawthorn/Bueb	Jaguar
2.	Valenzano/Musso	Maserati
3.	Collins/Frere	Aston-Martin
4.	Rolt/Hamilton	Jaguar
5.	Swaters/Claes	Jaguar
6.	Polensky/Frankenberg	Porsche
7.	Glockler/Juhan	Porsche
8.	Wilson/Mayers	Bristol
9.	Keen/Line	Bristol
10.	Seidel/Gendebien	Porsche

For the first time the amazingly fast $1\frac{1}{2}$ litre Porsches had appeared amongst the first six.

146

But the position based on the index of performance handicap was much more interesting. Darkness was favouring the smaller cars and now the imminent rain was to give them a further advantage.

		Engine capacity
1.	Jaguar	3,442
2.	Porsche	1,498
3.	Jaguar	3,442
4.	Maserati	2,991
5.	Porsche	1,498
6.	Aston-Martin	2,992
7.	Jaguar	3,442
8.	Porsche	1,498
9.	Deutsche-Bonnet Panhard	745
10.	Bristol	1,979

In the pits, folding chairs and beds where team staff had taken turns to doze were packed away. The timekeepers and lap chart scorers fortified themselves for the next twelve hours with cups of hot, strong tea or coffee.

Down at White House the dawn chorus was a half-hearted affair. A drove of sparrows who had tried out a few tentative chirps fled in terror as Rolt's Jaguar burst through the bend. A hovering hawk made one quick swoop, then changed its mind. The M.G. which had overturned and burnt itself out lay on its side in the ditch.

This year the ugly mist which sometimes rises at this point did not materialise. Instead it began to drizzle.

This was an anti-climax in the fullest sense of the word. As day strengthened, the inhabitants of Le Mans drifted back to watch the finish of their Grand Prix, but now it was to stand silently with hunched shoulders. The grandstands did not fill up again. The papers had the story of the accident and were making the most of it. The death-roll had risen to seventy. Whole pages were covered with grotesquely enlarged photographs of corpses and dismembered bodies. Did some editors who were far from the scene print their stories and pictures with more than a touch of relish?

By 8.0 a.m. only twenty-five cars were left out of the sixty which had started in the brightness of Saturday afternoon. The Rolt/Hamilton Jaguar had been withdrawn at dawn. Its gearbox had seized.

The order at three-quarter distance:

1.	Hawthorn/Bueb	Jaguar	234 laps
2.	Valenzano/Musso	Maserati	231 ,,
3.	Collins/Frere	Aston-Martin	231 ,,
4.	Swaters/Claes	Jaguar	227 ,,
5.	Polensky/Frankenberg	Porsche	216 ,,
6.	Wilson/Mayers	Bristol	211 ,,
7.	Glockler/Juhan	Porsche	210 ,,
8.	Keen/Line	Bristol	209 ,,
9.	Seidel/Gendebien	Porsche	209 ,,
10.	Wisdom/Fairman	Bristol	205 ,,

Now at last the Porsche of Polensky and Frankenberg had ousted the Jaguar from the leadership on handicap. As the rain increased so did the Porsche's advantage.

The restraint and steadiness of the Bristols was being rewarded. Their drivers were taking their machines through Indianapolis and Arnage as carefully as a housewife out for her morning's shopping.

At 10.0 the rain came down in earnest and did not relent till the end of the affair.

Two of the cars in this procession had been racing. During the last hours of darkness and the first of daylight the Aston-Martin driven by Collins and Frere had advanced to challenge the Musso/Valenzano Maserati for second position. Driving as steadily as a train on the soaked road

Paul Frere mastered the Maserati and even began to gain on the leading Jaguar. His three-lap deficit meant only 25 miles with the equivalent of London to Edinburgh and back still to travel. At that point Hawthorn took over the Jaguar and in the next hour put the matter beyond doubt. The Maserati's transmission succumbed and it joined the other dead cars.

That was virtually the end of the race. The Jaguar was unassailable and the rest of the cars well spaced out. It was not worth while for anyone to take undue risks. Yet the treacherous slipperiness of the road and the brittle nerviness of the crowd were sharply demonstrated soon after midday. Gendebien on his 1,500 c.c. rear-engined Porsche went past the grandstands trailing behind him the usual cloud of spray. He left his braking too late and as he went out of sight through the Dunlop bridge he was seen to be in the grip of a triple spin. The warning flags came out, the apathetic watchers in the stands stood up and men started running. The thought of another wrecked car with all its new implications was unbearable. However this time the safety barrier had stopped the gyrating Porsche. Gendebien, a sadder and wiser man, was able to bring his car round to the pits and hand over to his co-driver Seidel.

The clock-hands crept from midday to 3.40 while the Jaguar travelled over 350 miles. Lap after lap it rushed up the straight from White House, looking more like a speed-boat than a car, and slammed between grandstands and pits. The harsh crackle of its exhaust on the over-run echoed like machine-gun fire from the concrete walls and empty stands. Considering the conditions it was travelling very fast. By comparison the Triumphs were quiet, as they sailed past with a splash and a whistle.

The twenty-one surviving drivers were drinking the rain that trickled down their faces. Up on the roof of the grandstand the television man was attempting to follow the cars with his lens as they passed below him at two miles a minute. His antics would have made a gorilla in a tree look clumsy.

To watch the finish I went back to the spot from which I had watched the start. It was all very different now. Instead of sunshine, relentless rain; instead of the gay excited crowd, rows of silent, mournful people; instead of music between the announcements a silence that left too much room for thought.

All the usual receptions and parties in the pits and the marquees behind them had been cancelled. To add to the gloom we were told that the dead numbered nearly eighty.

Bueb called at the Jaguar pit to hand the car over to Hawthorn. The second driver had performed wonders in his first race with a big car, but it was right for Hawthorn to take the chequered flag. After the accident the race had little relish for him, but his team orders were to carry on. His victory was a great achievement both morally and technically.

Just before four a tall, sad figure walked down the road with the chequered flag in his hand. It was Charles Faroux, who had seen his life's dream turn to nightmare. Number 6, the winning car, passed by with its trail of spray and disappeared to start its last circuit. The clock hands came up and touched the twenty-fourth hour. Charles Faroux held up his flag. Down the road came the group of cars which had been loitering along so as to cross the line just after four. The Bristols had formed up to finish in the order of their team numbers: 32, 33, 34, followed by the Frazer-Nash number 35. The three astonishing Porsches sailed in to fourth, fifth and sixth places.

Almost last of all the dark green Jaguar came driving up

the middle of the road. Charles Faroux dipped his flag and Hawthorn raised his hand in acknowledgment.

The race was over.

Now for the first time in twenty-four hours the shining stretch of road that led down to White House was deserted. Its silence, wetness and emptiness brought an overwhelming sense of desolation. The race had ended, and with it a whole era of motor sport.[1]

OFFICIAL RESULTS

	Driver	Make	Distance in Kilometres
1.	Hawthorn/Bueb	Jaguar	4,175 (2,595 miles at 107·072 m.p.h.)
2.	Collins/Frere	Aston-Martin	4,073 (2,531 miles at 105·462 m.p.h.)
3.	Claes/Swaters	Jaguar	3,987
4.	Polensky/Von Frankenberg	Porsche	3,830
5.	Seidel/Gendebien	Porsche	3,716
6.	Glockler/Juhan	Porsche	3,680
7.	Wilson/Mayers	Bristol	3,654
8.	Keen/Line	Bristol	3,641
9.	Wisdom/Fairman	Bristol	3,614
10.	Becquart/Stoop	Frazer-Nash	3,506
11.	Cabianca/Sgorbati	Osca	3,449
12.	Miles/Lockett	M.G.	3,354
13.	Duntov/Veuillet	Porsche	3,304
14.	Dickson/Sanderson	Triumph	3,263
15.	Richardson/Haddley	Triumph	3,263
16.	Cornet/Mougin	D.B. Panhard	3,178
17.	Lund/Waeffler	M.G.	3,156
18.	Olivier/Jeser	Porsche	3,155
19.	Brooke/Morris Goodall	Triumph	2,886
20.	Héry/Trouis	D.B. Panhard	2,815
21.	Wadsworth/Brown	Cooper	2,790

[1] Le Mans in previous years was very different. Please read " Le Mans 1954 " by the staff of The Motor. (Temple Press.)

INDEX OF PERFORMANCE

1. Polensky/Von Frankenberg   Porsche
2. Hawthorn/Bueb   Jaguar
3. Collins/Frere   Aston-Martin
4. Seidel/Gendebien   Porsche
5. Glockler/Juhan   Porsche
6. Claes/Swaters   Jaguar
7. Cornet/Mougin   D.B. Panhard
8. Keen/Line   Bristol
9. Wisdom/Fairman   Bristol
10. Duntov/Veuillet   Porsche

CLASS WINNERS

Cubic Capacity	Driver	Car
Over 3,000 c.c.	Hawthorn/Bueb	Jaguar
Over 2,000 c.c.	Collins/Frere	Aston-Martin
Over 1,500 c.c.	Wilson/Mayers	Bristol
Over 1,000 c.c.	Polensky/Von Frankenberg	Porsche
Over 750 c.c.	Duntov/Veuillet	Porsche
Up to 750 c.c.	Héry/Trouis	D.B. Panhard

SPEEDS REGISTERED ON MULSANNE STRAIGHT OVER THE MEASURED KILOMETRE

Make	Speed in m.p.h.	Engine size
Mercedes-Benz	181·57	2·9 litres
Ferrari	175·60	4·4 ,,
Jaguar	173·94	3·5 ,,
Aston-Martin	155·60	2·9 ,,
Maserati	154·49	2·9 ,,
Ferrari	153·85	3·0 ,,
Gordini	140·85	2·0 ,,
Porsche	139·45	1·5 ,,
Bristol	138·43	2·0 ,,
Connaught	135·57	1·5 ,,
Osca	128·63	1·5 ,,
Frazer-Nash	128·63	2·0 ,,
Cooper-Climax	128·63	1·1 ,,

Make	Speed in m.p.h.	Engine size	
Panhard	118·69	0·8	,,
Porsche	118·07	1·1	,,
M.G.	117·69	1·5	,,
Salmson	117·44	2·3	,,
Triumph	113·09	2·0	,,
D.B. Panhard	106·26	0·7	,,
Constantin	105·82	2·0	,,

CHAPTER SIX

THE CONTINENT COMES
TO BRITAIN

British Grand Prix. Aintree. 16 July

THE DISASTER at Le Mans, reported with grim relish in all its terrible details, became at once a matter of international concern. The organisers of motor races were treated rather like wanton boys who had been discovered playing with an unexploded bomb and were severely cautioned. Governments awoke to the fact that they had completely shelved their responsibilities towards this most virile sport and made up for lost time by rapid and sometimes ill-considered measures. Other concerns were able to make convenient readjustments to their plans under the pious cloak of desire for public safety. The French Government banned all motor racing indefinitely. The Italian followed suit but quickly revised its opinion and adopted a more realistic attitude. The Swiss Grand Prix was cancelled and shortly came the news that the German Grand Prix, although it was to be held on a course specially constructed for motor racing, would not take place. In the House of Commons a Member asked whether the Government considered adopting measures to protect spectators at motor races. Sir Lucas Tooth, in reply, stated that since the matter was under review by the R.A.C. the Government saw no reason to interfere.

From a Government which has been often slated for its unimaginative attitude towards motor racing, this was a

sane and reasonable answer. Even at that very moment the
R.A.C. were going ahead with plans for their 10th Grand
Prix. In Britain all motor racing is controlled by the R.A.C.,
though they delegate the actual organisation of meetings to
one or other of the clubs.

Grands Prix held at Silverstone since the war have been
organised by the British Racing Drivers' Club, whose
President-in-Chief is The Duke of Edinburgh. In 1955 the
R.A.C. decided to switch the classic British race to the
North of England, to the new Aintree course, where races
are organised by the British Automobile Racing Club.

Virtually speaking, the British Grand Prix has only come
into being since the war. Away back in 1926 the R.A.C.,
inspired by the great French event, organised their first
Grand Prix at Brooklands. Since the law did not—and still
does not—allow public roads to be closed for racing, this
great autodrome near Weybridge had become the centre of
British motor sport. With its high concrete banking and
famous bumps it was the scene of dramatic events which
deserve a history in themselves. But it bore little resemblance
to the usual Grand Prix circuit, even though the organisers
arranged chicanes to simulate corners. That first race was
won by the Frenchmen Senechal and Wagner in a Delage.
They averaged 71·61 m.p.h. over the 287 miles and were
followed by Sir Malcolm Campbell in a Bugatti. The next
year the Delage team swept the board; first Benoist, second
Bourcher, third Divo. The average had gone up to 85·6
m.p.h.—a speed almost identical with the winning speed of
the 1955 Grand Prix, though achieved under entirely
different circumstances. After this event the R.A.C. put
up the shutters and the British Grand Prix was not held
again until more than twenty years later.

From 1935 to 1938 races which almost had the status of a
Grand Prix were held at Donington Park. This course had

been constructed in a private park to meet the urgent need for a road circuit. It saw triumphs by some of the great figures of motor racing: Rosemeyer, Seaman, Nuvolari. In 1937 and '38 the Auto-Union and Mercedes-Benz teams came over to show the British what German genius and thoroughness could achieve. They left behind them a sense of inferiority which did little to strengthen national morale in the 1938 panic.

The Government took over both Brooklands and Donington on the outbreak of war. Certainly they were no longer required for racing. Too many of those lovers of speed were in the R.A.F. And in September of 1940, when Western Civilisation hung by a hair, it was saved by the very type of young man who had caused eyebrows to rise when he bounced past in his rather noisy little sports car.

When the war was over the Government declined to hand back Brooklands and Donington. They have not done so yet. No doubt they have their reasons.

Just at the moment when races were reviving all over Europe and the British motor industry was entering its most glorious period, the sport had been dealt a cruel blow. Faced with the complete extinction of motor racing in Britain, the R.A.C. took the desperate but courageous measure of acquiring the aerodrome of Silverstone with its ready-made runways and perimeter tracks. This bald and barren plateau 80 miles from London has been the centre of British racing for seven years. It has never got to look like anything but an abandoned airfield. The four winds of heaven take turns to sweep it. When the inevitable rain comes the grass is turned into squelchy mud. So inadequate were the communications in the early days that to see his racing the Londoner had to get up before daylight and if he was badly placed in the car-park he reached home well after dark.

Yet this sport attracts so great and enthusiastic a following that all the big meetings have drawn huge crowds. The Grand Prix, of course, was always the most powerful magnet, although it has never until now been won by either a British car or a British driver.

From 1948 to 1954 this Grand Prix saw an unbroken series of successes by Italian cars. 1948 was notable for the first appearance in Britain of Ascari, then driving for Maserati. The winner that year was his team-mate and teacher Villoresi, but Ascari followed him into second place. In 1949 a Maserati again won, driven this time by the Swiss de Graffenried. But the real sensation of the race was the appearance in second place of the twelve year old British E.R.A., prepared and driven by F. R. Gerard. In the whole history of Grand Prix racing only one achievement by a car of British make surpassed Gerard's second place with this old car. That was when Sir Henry Segrave won the 1924 San Sebastian Grand Prix in a works Sunbeam.

In 1950 the British event also bore the title of European Grand Prix, and the race was honoured by the presence of the King and Queen. Alas, they came to witness another foreign triumph. The much heralded British Racing Motor, or B.R.M., was only able to manage a demonstration run. The Alfa-Romeo team was irresistible. First was Farina, second Fagioli and third the British driver Parnell. Since that day a reigning monarch has not attended the classic British motoring event.

1951 was significant because it was the first contest in which the new Ferraris ousted the Alfa-Romeos. It also showed how rich the Argentine was in racing talent. Gonzalez, who was to become a gigantic figure at Silverstone, hurled his Ferrari round in practice to record a lap at over 100 m.p.h. In the race itself he managed to stay on the road till the end and won at 96·11 m.p.h. This still stands as the highest average at which this Grand Prix has been won. Second to Gonzalez was a driver who was fast coming to the fore in European racing—J. M. Fangio.

In 1952 and '53, like the other principal events on the calendar, the race was run under Formula Two. Alberto Ascari, on his way to becoming World Champion, was Ferrari's number one driver. He took the trophy in both those years at speeds of 90·92 and 92·97 m.p.h. respectively. 1952 was noteworthy for two reasons. Firstly, because the B.B.C. covered it very thoroughly for television. Unfortunately the use of telephoto lenses entirely killed the impression of speed and the cars appeared on the screen to be moving at a snail's pace. It must have given many people who have never seen a race a completely false impression. Secondly, because another astounding performance was put up by a British driver in a comparatively slow car. This time it was the hitherto unknown J. M. Hawthorn who finished in third place at the wheel of his Cooper-Bristol. Many forecast that this young man had a great future ahead of him.

1954 was enlivened by the presence of two of the revolutionary new Mercedes-Benz. It was only their second appearance and they were still in the streamlined shape in which they had triumphed at Rheims. Their drivers were Fangio and Kling. Even during practice it was clear that they were not suited to this circuit. The high curves enclosing the wheels prevented even Fangio from seeing the ridiculous oildrums used as markers at Silverstone. He sent several of them flying and the dents in his Mercedes provided much material for the Press. In the race itself Gonzalez bundled his Ferrari into the lead the instant the flag dropped. He seemed to lift the car foward by sheer determination and fairly smacked up through the gears. He never stopped and never lost his lead. Fangio chased him courageously for half the race but his car was unstable and his engine sickly. He gradually fell back to fourth.

Behind Gonzalez a fine duel developed between Moss and Hawthorn. For the first time both these expert British drivers were matched on cars of similar performance. Everyone was anxious to gather more material for the eternal argument as to which is the better driver. Moss proved himself surer, smoother and faster. He gradually drew away from Hawthorn only to be put out of the race twenty laps from the end when his machine failed him.

Followed now by his own team-mate, Gonzalez was able to slow down considerably. His final average was 86·69 m.p.h. This was the seventh consecutive win by an Italian car and the fourth consecutive win by Ferrari.

The 1955 British Grand Prix was the first full-scale event to be held since Le Mans. The B.A.R.C., therefore, found themselves in the position of having to organise their first Grande Epreuve with the eyes of the entire motoring world upon them. On the Continent, Government Departments, Conventions of Motoring Organisations, Editors of Weekly Papers and most of the men in the street were arguing as to whether motor racing had become too dangerous to be tolerated. Meanwhile the answer was quietly being prepared at Aintree.

Aintree stands a few miles outside Liverpool. Everyone knows it as the home of the Grand National. A year or two ago its owner, Mrs. Topham, decided to advance with the times and construct a circuit for car racing. The track was planned to run alongside the steeplechase course, now inside and now outside it. It could thus take advantage of the splendid grandstand accommodation and all the other amenities for spectators. During the winter of 1953-4 the work was carried out at a cost of over £100,000, and racing

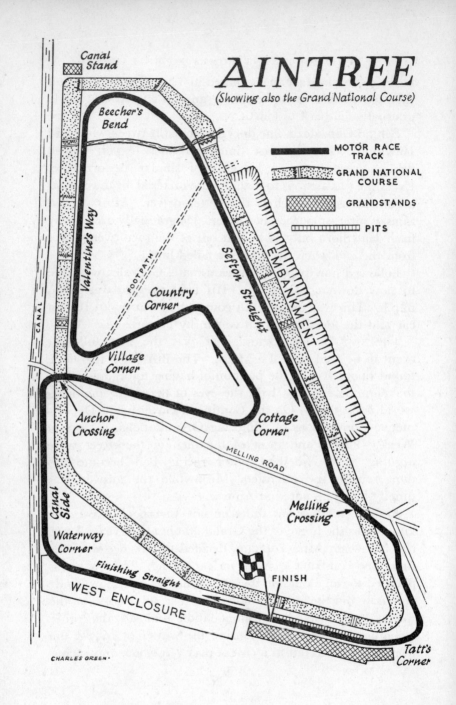

AINTREE

(Showing also the Grand National Course)

Canal Stand

Beecher's Bend

Valentine's Way

CANAL

FOOTPATH

Country Corner

Village Corner

Sefton Straight

EMBANKMENT

MOTOR RACE TRACK

GRAND NATIONAL COURSE

GRANDSTANDS

PITS

Anchor Crossing

Cottage Corner

MELLING ROAD

Melling Crossing

Canal Side

Waterway Corner

Finishing Straight

FINISH

WEST ENCLOSURE

Tatt's Corner

CHARLES GREEN.

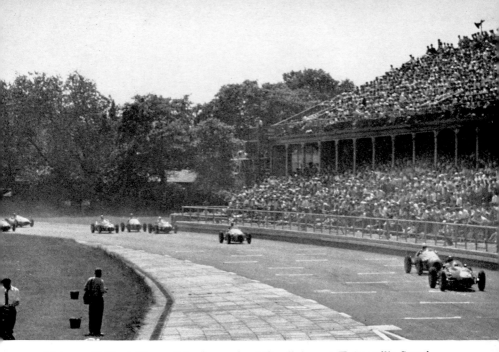

Aintree.   Collins' Maserati leads a pair of Gordinis past Tattersall's Stand
(Photo Klemantaski)

Aintree.   Hawthorn in a works Ferrari shows Collins the way round Tatt's
Corner.   In the background the Grand National course   *(Photo March)*

Aintree. Hard in pursuit of Fangio, Moss squeezes past McAlpine on the entry to Tatt's Corner. No. 32 is one of the streamlined British Connaughts
(Photo March)

Aintree. Before the vast crowd on the Embankment Schell takes a determined grip on the Vanwall as he enters Melling Crossing
(Photo Klemantaski)

began during the following season. Although true road racing may not be seen in Britain, the three-mile Aintree circuit is a very close equivalent. It was laid down and built exactly like the standard thirty-five foot highway. Its seven corners and one wiggly section make it an excellent test of driving skill. Sheer speed does not count for so much here. Even on the straight the fastest cars do not expect to reach more than 150 m.p.h. The width and surface of the road is uniform the whole way round. There are no bumps, kerbstones or drain holes. The result is that each corner can be taken as its shape indicates without regard for local peculiarities.

Since this race was to be held so soon after Le Mans, and a large crowd was expected, the safety precautions were of interest. There were twelve observer posts round the three-mile circuit. At each of them was a doctor and team of ambulance men. In addition, there were ambulance men at other points. Four ambulances were in strategic positions on the circuit, and firemen with apparatus were at the corners and at all the observer posts. Even these duty personnel were protected by concrete barriers. They were instructed not to congregate in groups, to keep behind barriers and never to stand with their backs to the cars. On race day itself there were policemen—calm, tolerant and good-humoured policemen in shirt sleeves—who got the people to do what they wanted without blowing whistles or waving their arms.

Such were the precautions lest an accident should happen. Other measures had been taken to make it almost impossible for a spectator to be injured by a competitor. The spectators were contained in three main areas, all on the outside of the course. To understand their position it is best to visualise them from the point of view of a driver going round the circuit. Leaving the start he soon has on his left the West

Enclosure. A good fifty feet of open space lie between the road proper and the enclosure. In that space he can cope with most eventualities. Should he by any mischance reach the enclosure he will be stopped by strips of reinforced concrete mounted on concrete posts and protected in front by thick straw bales. Once past that enclosure there is a high wall on his right and beyond it the canal. As he goes through the loop no spectators are near him. On the short straight before the canal turn he sees people on his left, but he will have to cross the Grand National course and swim the canal to reach them.

The main bulk of watchers is contained in the big embankment. Here there is room for 100,000 at five shillings a time. They command a fine view of the straight and of the two corners in the loop. They are absolutely safe, for the Grand National course separates them from the roadway. Once again in the tricky winding section before Tatt's Corner there are no spectators. The grandstands are set well back from the road. Even though the track is sunken and lined by a solid wall, no spectators are allowed within twenty feet of the roadside. The result is that everyone has a wider view of the racing and can appreciate the driving far better than if they were crammed up against the road. This was not a radical new measure never before contemplated. The provision of a margin for error has always been an axiom of race organisers in this country.

Only in one place did the width of road available to the car travelling at full speed narrow from 35 to 32 feet. This was in front of the pits. In reality the roadway here is wider, but a yellow line had been painted on it to ensure that a double lane was available for cars calling at their pits. Drivers who wished to stop had to pull inside it as soon as they came round Tatt's Corner. Failure to respect this line meant that the black flag would be shown to the offender, who would have to stop and listen to what the Chief Marshal had to say about him.

Nowhere on the Aintree course is the driver trapped by the crowd or forced into a bottleneck. At all the corners he has plenty of opportunity to escape and kill his speed harmlessly in some open space. The most closed-in portion is that between Melling Crossing and Tatt's Corner. This is taken at 100 m.p.h., with quick bursts of throttle to provoke the correct degree of drift. An error of judgment at the beginning of the wiggle means that the driver will be in serious difficulties by the end of it. But, as Jean Behra remarked during practice, a driver knows he can only kill himself. He does not have the awful feeling that when he goes out of control he will smash into a crowd.

In fact the foreign drivers expressed themselves as very happy about the Aintree circuit. They, perhaps more than anyone else, appreciated the precautions taken to safeguard spectators. They found the course interesting, though some of them said they would have preferred a series of faster bends instead of the four slow corners of the loop.

Aintree was already a happy hunting ground for Moss. He had won several victories there in his private Maserati during the 1954 season. He held the lap record in 2 minutes 0·6 seconds, a speed of 89·55 m.p.h. This seemed to be one place where Moss's bad luck could not touch him.

During practice many drivers declared that Moss's speed was no longer possible for cars of the present Formula. Low boards had been placed at the corners so that they could not be clipped too close. They made just that fraction of a difference. None the less, Moss equalled his own record. Fangio could not get within a second of him and Jean Behra in the fastest Maserati was two seconds slower. On Friday Fangio reckoned he knew the course well enough to make his bid. He equalled the record but Moss did better,

BRITISH GRAND PRIX

ENTRY LIST

Driver				Car
Behra	..	..	..	.. Maserati
Musso	..	..	..	.. Maserati
Mieres	..	..	..	.. Maserati
Perdisa	..	..	..	.. Maserati
Fangio	..	..	..	.. Mercedes-Benz
Moss	..	..	..	.. Mercedes-Benz
Kling	..	..	..	.. Mercedes-Benz
Taruffi	..	..	..	.. Mercedes-Benz
Hawthorn		..	..	.. Ferrari
Trintignant		..	..	.. Ferrari
Castellotti		..	..	.. Ferrari
Manzon	..	..	..	.. Gordini
da Silva Ramos			..	.. Gordini
Sparken	..	..	..	.. Gordini
Wharton	..	..	..	... Vanwall
Schell	..	..	..	.. Vanwall
McAlpine		..	..	.. Connaught
Fairman	..	..	..	.. Connaught
Rolt	..	..	..	.. Connaught
Marr	..	..	..	.. Connaught
Brabham		..	..	.. Cooper
Collins	..	..	..	.. Maserati
Salvadori	..	..	..	.. Maserati
Macklin	..	..	..	.. Maserati
Gould	..	..	..	.. Maserati

and clocked 2 minutes 0·4 seconds. Though he tried all the cars including Moss's, Fangio could not equal that time.

This practice session was a real test of merit. In view of the way in which the race itself finished it was as well that Moss had previously established himself as the fastest man over the circuit.

*   *   *

The B.A.R.C. deserved sunshine for their big day and they got it. Friday's rosy sunset was no false prophet. Racing was due to begin at eleven o'clock and from early morning people were flocking from all over the North of England to the racecourse. This was the first time that the enthusiasts of the North had seen a true Grand Prix on their own ground. Liverpool itself was crammed that week-end. The motor race coincided with the Liverpool Show of Prize Livestock, and in addition Princess Margaret was to visit Southport on the same Saturday. On Friday evening the streets had been full of people who had come up late from London and were searching in vain for hotel accommodation.

The course itself wore an air of authoritative glamour. The confident crescent of grandstands that have witnessed innumerable Grand Nationals lent some of their tradition to this new race. After all, both races have the same basis —man and his mount. If the horses' lap record was 28·75 m.p.h., and the car record 89·55, the difference was purely relative. To-day mown grass lay on the Grand National course and the famous jumps looked scraggy and untrimmed. But there was an unmistakable aroma of horse about the area back of the grandstands where notices pointed to Paddock, Saddling Enclosure, Jockey's Room. The spirits of Lottery, Troytown, and Golden Miller may well have roamed unseen and unheard, for the click of a ghostly hoof would have been drowned by the sound of engines warming up near by.

Something of the Continent had come to Britain that day and merged with certain discomforts that were unmistakably English. A vast and record crowd was present, its 150,000 surpassing the record for the Grand National itself. The grandstands had been sold out weeks before. Throughout the morning the Embankment with its capacity for 100,000 gradually filled up. Seen from afar it was a mass of almost unbroken white, evidence of the English male's preference for a white shirt. Above on tall poles the flags of the competing nations hung limply on the still air. One of the B.A.R.C. officials glanced at them.

" We could have done with a little wind to straighten them out."

It was the only detail on which the race organisation had fallen short of perfection.

A programme of races had been arranged for the delight of the spectators, but it had been wisely limited to three. In the event it was to produce a series of results unique in motoring sport.

Well before eleven the machines that were to contest the first race were being pushed out into the paddock, which is well placed in front of the stands so that everyone can see the cars. They were tiny racing cars with engines of no more than 500 c.c. capacity—the size of a large motor cycle's engine. 500 c.c. racing has become the most important element in British motor sport since the war. These little machines can be produced at a fraction of the cost of a Grand Prix car. As a result racing has come within the reach of a great many more men. 500 c.c. races have been the nursery where new drivers have learned the tricks of the trade and from which some of our best drivers have emerged—among them Stirling Moss himself. Let it not be imagined, though, that driving such cars is child's play. They are capable of 120 m.p.h., and can be cornered at remarkably high speeds. The competitors duel fiercely among themselves. Shunting, carving, slip-streaming, bumping and boring are all the order of the day.

When they were sent on their way sharply at 11.00 the air was rent by the dry, penetrating crackle of their mega-phone-shaped exhausts. The 17-lap race resolved itself into a close struggle between Russell and Lewis-Evans, both on Cooper-Nortons. So well matched were the cars that as they careered along the straight the drivers tucked their heads down out of the wind and even seemed to be trying to urge their cars on with forward jerks of their shoulders. The only way to gain an advantage was to go round the corners faster and that was how Russell managed to scrape home $4\frac{1}{2}$ seconds to the good. Anyone who had been inclined to scoff at the tiny cars was sobered when the race average was given as 78·19 and Russell's record lap at 79·53. His time of 2 minutes 15·8 seconds was only 3 seconds slower than the third Gordini's best time in the Grand Prix practice.

Before the 500 race had finished the gleaming selection of purchasable cars was assembled ready in the paddock to do battle in the Sports Car Race. Five of the finned " D " type Jaguars, of which only Hawthorn's was a factory entry, were matched against four factory Aston-Martins and twenty other cars competing for sundry awards. At the end of the first rushing lap Hawthorn led, but he was passed successively by the Aston-Martins of Salvadori, Collins, Parnell and Walker. They took the chequered flag in that order. Once again the lap record was broken, this time by Peter Collins with a speed of 83·33 m.p.h. His 2 minutes 9·6 seconds was better than the practice times of half a dozen Grand Prix cars, but remember that his car had a 3 litre engine as against their 2½.

Everyone's appetite was now thoroughly whetted, so the B.A.R.C. gave them time to eat their lunch in peace and work up their anticipation for the Grand Prix. One of the great advantages of the Aintree course is the creature comforts it offers. There are plenty of bars and restaurants and places where you can sit down. Thousands of chickens had died that the Aintree crowd might eat, which it did with relish and a liberal portion of ale.

Meanwhile the mechanics had wheeled the Grand Prix cars out to the front of the pits and the munching multitude was regaled with the blip of tuned engines. In the paddock twenty cream Austin-Healey two-seaters were lined up, each with the flag of a nation on its mudguard and a nice new R.A.C. badge on its front. A Parade of Drivers was to take place.

Just an hour before the race was due to begin the procession began. Each famous driver sat on the back of the car with his feet on the seat cushion and was driven slowly down on to the road and away round the circuit at 20 m.p.h. Each one was named by the announcer, but for the people around the circuit it was hard to recognise them. They looked so completely different without the helmet and goggles in which they are so often photographed. Heads bare, they seemed very much more human.

One figure was too well known to be mistaken. As Fangio's car moved slowly down the long straight before the hundred thousand on the embankment they suddenly broke ranks. Across the sacred turf of the Grand National course they poured and stopped the Champion's car. The road was a mob of excited, admiring people. Not till a great many autograph books had been signed was the cavalcade able to move on again.

The Parade had taken longer than was expected and the Grand Prix, the announcer insisted, would start On Time. Cars were hastily pushed out to drive round the circuit and take up positions on the starting grid.

MOSS Mercedes	FANGIO Mercedes	BEHRA Maserati
KLING Mercedes		TARUFFI Mercedes
MIERES Maserati	SCHELL Vanwall	SIMON Maserati
MUSSO Maserati	CASTELLOTTI Ferrari	
MANZON Gordini	HAWTHORN Ferrari	TRINTIGNANT Ferrari
ROLT Connaught	WHARTON Vanwall	
MACKLIN Maserati	McALPINE Connaught	DA SILVA RAMOS Gordini
MARR Connaught	SALVADORI Maserati	
	GOULD Maserati	SPARKEN Gordini
COLLINS Maserati	BRABHAM Cooper	

Nine motor horns in yoke let forth their ghastly shriek from the roof of the pits. Ten minutes to go.

Eight minutes later came one of those unforgettable moments which occur quite by chance and which give to ordinary events a depth of meaning which you do not expect. Into the middle of the wild bustle, roaring and confusion that always precedes a Grand Prix start came the warning drum-roll of the National Anthem. The men and women in the stands rose to their feet, the crowd in the West Enclosure and the multitude on the Embankment rose. Conversations were cut off abruptly and those who had

169

come from abroad gazed about them in surprise. A French mechanic silenced his engine and slowly straightened up. One young Italian driver visiting England for the first time looked as embarrassed as a man who has strayed into the wrong church. He looked round for a cue from some of his older compatriots.

The quiet music went out over the tarmac and the mown grass. The hundred and fifty thousand people made no more sound than the grass on a lonely hill and they were far stiller.

It was over quickly and the mood was killed with sudden urgency. The chorus of horns proclaimed that the start was only a minute away. With a stroke of showmanship that was genius someone sent forth over the loudspeakers a burst of the Coronation Fanfare. There was just time for the echoing brass chords to awaken their unforgettable response when a new and deafening sound drowned them completely.

Engines were being started. Drivers hurried to climb into their cars, mechanics ran to be clear of the starting grid before the flag fell.

Nothing equals the dramatic intensity of the moment before the start. It is something more than sport. It is as if men are going into battle, the gorgeous panoplied battle of lance and armour. The true poet of this century might write an ode about this moment. It would not be respected now because you just aren't supposed to see poetry in the start of a motor race. But in a thousand years time that poet would be the Juvenal of the twentieth century.

It was coincidence that the cars on the starting grid bore the same colours as the rival charioteers of ancient Rome—red, green, blue and white. Yet the charioteer with the reins of a team of maddened horses lashed to his hands finds his modern counterpart in the racing driver mounted in his projectile of steel, his life at the mercy of his skill. In

Rome that very day bulldozers were levelling the dusts of the deserted Circus Maximus. But at Aintree the crowds came to their feet when the cars leapt forward, sent on their way by the crosses of St. Patrick, St. Andrew and St. George.

From the moment that Fangio came round at the end of the first lap with Moss on his heels it seemed a foregone conclusion that one of these two would win the race. It was the familiar formation that had been seen at Monaco, Spa and Zandvoort. The only difference was that this time, since he was on his home ground, it might be Moss's turn to win. Yet as the race progressed it resolved itself into a number of personal duels which made it interesting until the end. Each of the Mercedes in turn disposed of its challenging Maserati until they were left in an unassailable position.

Even after two laps the field had strung out and the two leaders were well clear. The only man who was within striking distance was Jean Behra, but his Maserati was being pushed to the limit. Behind him came Kling, Taruffi, Mieres, Musso, Trintignant, Castellotti and Hawthorn. Rolt's Connaught, in fifteenth place, was the first British car. Immediately behind him were Schell and Wharton in the Vanwalls. Schell's car had stalled on the line and the mechanics had to run out to push him away. Since then he had been careering up through the field at a formidable speed, moving perhaps as fast as any car in the race.

Moss was within yards of Fangio's tail for the first two laps. On the third, as they came snaking through from Melling Crossing it was the English driver who led by 50 yards. One car was already out. André Simon's Maserati had retired with a broken gear selector.

After only ten laps the inter-make race was resolved. The gallant Behra's Maserati passed the stands with smoke pouring from its bonnet. An oil pipe had burst and he had to stop out on the circuit at Waterway. That was one

171

Maserati disposed of. As a result the Mercedes were in the first three positions. Mieres, however, had tucked himself behind Kling and was within inches of him at every corner. With a light and sure touch on the bends he made it look as if he could go past whenever he chose. Musso in his turn was trailing Taruffi in the fourth Mercedes and waiting for a chance to pass.

It was about this time that Rolt, having negotiated the first bend after Melling Crossing, took his foot off the accelerator to ease speed a little. No reaction. The throttle had jammed wide open. His passage through the ensuing bends was highly dramatic. Dust flew and the straw bales were lucky to be let off so lightly. With Tatt's Corner ahead Rolt took his only course and let the clutch out. The four-cylinder engine revved up to 8,500, but he managed to squeeze round the corner and pull in towards the pits.

Soon afterwards Marr, in one of the new streamlined Connaughts, spun at Anchor Corner. For a moment the bright green car stood dangerously athwart the road; then Marr reversed smartly on to the verge, waited till the pursuing cars had passed and accelerated away again.

The fast pace set by the leaders was playing havoc amongst the slower cars. From as early as the fifth lap Moss and Fangio had been catching them up. Six of them had to stop at the pits for adjustments and by the fifteenth lap two had definitely retired.

Fangio and Moss were driving with complete calm, sitting well back with arms at full stretch. Fangio was quietly chewing on something. On the sixteenth lap he stopped chewing and his mouth was set as he changed down for Cottage Corner with an aggressive movement of the gear lever. On lap seventeen he was in the lead. Moss's expression did not alter much, but he was careful not to let his man take a lead of more than a few yards. On the twenty-second lap Moss pulled out and attempted to pass Fangio on the Railway Straight. He drew level but could not pass before it was time to brake for Melling Crossing. On the following lap exactly the same thing happened. Fangio had no intention of giving anything away though Moss was nosing up to him on every corner. On the twenty-fourth lap they were both catching up with Trintignant and about to lap him. Fangio came down the straight very fast. It looked as if he would pass Trintignant and Moss would be cut off behind him through the winding approach to Tatt's. At the last moment Fangio decided he could not make it and drew in behind the red car. The three machines attacked Tatt's Corner almost together. Moss nipped past Fangio on the inside but found himself baulked by Trintignant. Rather than cut in front of his team-mate he braked and let Fangio pass into the lead again.

His reward came during the next lap. Exerting full power as he came out of the long canal turn he caught Fangio on the straight and managed to pass him just in time to take Melling Crossing at a reasonable speed. After that he was in the lead for the rest of the race, driving with complete mastery of the car and the relaxed grace which makes his style completely individual. The speed instead of falling continued to rise steadily.

At 30 laps only 17 cars were left. Mieres and Musso in their Maseratis were the only ones who were capable of challenging the Mercedes. Across the centre of the course came walking an irrepressibly gay figure in blue overalls swinging his crash helmet by the strap. It was Harry Schell. His brilliant drive had ended when his throttle linkage snapped. But his day was by no means done.

After 40 laps only 14 cars were still going, out of an original field of 24. The leader's average had risen to 86·85 m.p.h. In the duels for third and fifth places Kling, who never likes to have a car on his tail, had increased his lead over Mieres to 3 seconds. Musso, on the other hand, had at last got the better of Taruffi and was 4 seconds in front of him. These two duels between the very well matched Mercedes and Maseratis emphasised how much the German company owe to their two master drivers. Although mounted on similar cars they were a clear minute ahead.

Neubauer, their team manager, now put out this cryptic signal:

```
┌──────────────────┐
│  110   MIER      │
│    R.   G.       │
└──────────────────┘
```

This showed the leaders that they were a minute ahead of the nearest challenger, Mieres, and that they could play for safety. There was no point in Fangio and Moss duelling when the race was in the pocket of whichever of them put his foot down hardest. It is not easy to slow Moss down, however, and for the next 20 laps the average mounted gradually to 86·26—86·4—86·44—a remarkable display of regularity.

At 40 laps the order was:

1.	Moss	Mercedes	1 hr. 23 mins. 33 secs.
2.	Fangio	Mercedes	1 hr. 23 mins. 42·2 secs.
3.	Kling	Mercedes	1 hr. 24 mins. 29·2 secs.
4.	Mieres	Maserati	1 hr. 24 mins. 32·4 secs.
5.	Musso	Maserati	1 hr. 25 mins. 10·8 secs.
6.	Taruffi	Mercedes	1 hr. 25 mins. 14 secs.
7.	Hawthorn	Ferrari	} 39 laps
8.	Trintignant	Ferrari	
9.	Macklin	Maserati	} 38 laps
10.	Sparken	Gordini	

Only these ten cars were left in the race.

The forty-fifth lap was half distance.

Just then, when it might have seemed that the race was beginning to lack interest, began a series of events which brought new drama. One of the over-stressed cars had suffered an oil leak and distributed some of the slippery substance on the track. There was a nasty patch of it at Tatt's Corner. Lance Macklin had been circulating at a satisfactory speed in the Maserati belonging to Stirling Moss. It was in fact the very car which held the Aintree lap record. It had not been lucky this season. The superstitious Moss had decided to see if a change of colour would improve its luck and it appeared for the British Grand Prix painted a matt grey. The scrutineers insisted that as a British car it ought to be painted green, so a little gusset of sickly green was painted down the bonnet of number 46. Certainly the grey tones deceived the Moss gremlin that day, for it never found its way under the bonnet. But some little devil took a hold of the Maserati just as the leaders were out for their forty-sixth lap, and as it came out of Tatt's flicked it on the oil patch. The Maserati spun and whacked the straw bales guarding the end of Tattersall's Grandstand. Its tail was dented in, so Macklin walked in leisurely fashion back towards his pits. He was met by Alf Francis, Moss's former mechanic, and together they strolled down to take a look at the damaged car. The machine was deemed fit to continue its race so Macklin climbed in and drove on again —eventually to finish eighth. Such are the rewards of keeping going in a race of elimination.

The second Vanwall, driven up till then by Wharton, was now in at its pit. While Wharton strolled up and down the roadway Schell acted as fag to the mechanics, and ran to fetch them tools from the pit-counter while they worked on the engine. He'd tasted a sample of the Vanwall's speed and was keen to have another drive in Wharton's car. His enthusiasm affected the mechanics, and they worked to put the car on the road again. Moss and Fangio had passed perhaps fifteen times while the green car stood motionless at its pits. But before the last bolt was screwed home Schell was ready with his helmet on. He rejoined the fray with as much gusto as if he were only half a lap behind the leaders.

Meanwhile Hawthorn had come in to his pit. He was feeling the effects of the heat. Castellotti was already out of the race with engine trouble. He was more than willing to take over Hawthorn's car, so number 16 was soon away with a new driver. Smoke trailed from its rear tyres as the Italian made an over-enthusiastic get-away.

Now superior engineering had begun to tell in the duel between Kling and Mieres. The Maserati came down the straight leaving a long cloud of blue smoke behind it. Mieres pulled into the Maserati pit. The engine was bathed in oil and the cockpit was flooded with it. Bitterly disappointed, Mieres climbed from the car. The second Maserati had retired.

Now only Musso in fourth place interrupted the Mercedes formation. At 45 laps he was one second in front of Taruffi. But Taruffi was the older and more experienced driver. He had not driven the Grand Prix Mercedes until two days before this race and he was still familiarising himself with it. He had been driving with that wise head of his, and taking a line on the corners that bore the unmistakable Taruffi signature. At 50 laps he was half a second behind Musso and ready to take him whenever he wanted. By lap 55 he was in front and yet another Maserati had been disposed of.

The Maserati pit manager observed Musso's valiant attempts to re-pass Taruffi and realised that they could only result in another wrecked engine. Musso was signalled to

Monza. Moss (16) makes his best start of the year and leads from Fangio (18) and Kling (20) at the fall of the flag *(Photo Associated Press)*

Monza. Castellotti driving at the limit of adhesion. The word " Prova " painted on the tail indicates that this Ferrari was intended only for practice *(Photo Klemantaski)*

Monza. Four Mercedes pursued by a Ferrari—Moss, Fangio, Taruffi, Kling,
Castellotti. Even in the early afternoon the sun cast long shadows on the
steeply inclined banking of the new track. The cars are travelling at about
170 miles an hour   *(Photo Keystone)*

keep his engine revolutions below 6,000. Maserati wanted at least one of their cars to finish the race.

Now, with 35 laps still to go Mercedes were in the happy position of occupying the first four places. Fangio and Moss had dealt with Behra, Kling with Mieres, and Taruffi had left Musso behind. Neubauer showed his drivers a signal which read:

```
Moss.
Fang.
Klin.
Taru.
Muss.
```

He followed it up with another bearing the mystic letters pi. *Piano* means " Take it easy " and to this invitation to go slower Fangio replied with a resigned gesture of the right hand. Moss had acknowledged every signal from the pit with the gracious nod of a Duchess. He was very happy.

On lap 61 the hapless Macklin was passed by three Mercedes. Taruffi had been lapped by Moss and Fangio, but now he decided that he knew his car well enough to stay with them. Though Moss's speed continued to rise frantically in spite of Neubauer's signals, Taruffi kept the leading cars in sight for lap after lap.

By now the official Maserati and Ferrari teams had each only one car left. Every British made car except one was out of the race. But what was this? In front of the grandstands Harry Schell had sailed past Sparken's Gordini and given the French driver a happy smile. In a less public place certain rude signals might have been made, for Schell was out to enjoy himself. Each time he passed the pits he gave the mechanics a cheery thumbs-up signal which clearly meant: " Thanks for getting me going again. The engine's fine." The Vanwall mechanics sat in a row on the pit-counter and swung their legs happily every time their car went by.

Schell was really out for blood. Not far in front of him was Castellotti on the surviving Ferrari. Gradually Schell drew closer until on the railway straight he passed the Italian car. Castellotti was not a man to take this lightly; he clung to Schell all the way round that lap and got past him again just before Becher's. It was no good. In a test of sheer speed Schell passed him again on the straight and once more shot past the grandstands in the lead. Though really laps behind, the Vanwall stayed in front of the Italian car and gradually drew away. When Moss and Fangio caught him up Schell gave way politely and then proceeded to demonstrate that the Vanwall was almost as fast as the German cars. He sailed round behind them for several laps and gave the crowd to wonder what might have happened if his throttle linkage had not broken in the early stages. The Vanwall was very fast.

The race speed was certainly not falling. Fangio was always within ten seconds of Moss and his face had the expression of a poker player. Even if the race was over and they were now driving to team orders, Moss did not want to let the unpredictable Argentine squeeze in front of him again. The progress of those two appeared to be purely mechanical. It required an effort of will to realise that they were going faster than ever before. In other races which Mercedes have won the average dropped once victory was assured. In Moss's race it rose and rose. He even broke his old lap record and achieved this additional honour which everyone had expected would go to Fangio. These were speeds which during the past weeks had caused people to raise their hands in horror and exclaim that man was no longer able to control his machines. Every corner was being taken at a velocity which the ordinary motorist would not

178

believe possible. Yet so easy did these drivers make their performance seem that some people were leaving to go home five laps before the end.

They missed a remarkable demonstration.

During the final laps Fangio closed the gap between himself and Moss. No one was quite sure what he might be capable of doing. He had led Moss over the line so many times. Could he bear to play second fiddle now? As Moss slowed for Tatt's Corner on the last lap of all Fangio came through the winding section after Melling Crossing like a cat with half its tail bitten off. His speed into the sharp bend seemed suicidal. Moss remained unperturbed and took the corner on his usual impeccable line. He had no intention of throwing the race away now. Immediately behind him Fangio was in a powerful slide which would have taken any other man into Macklin's straw bales. Not so Fangio. By sheer force and confidence he held his car to the middle of the road and even before the slide was finished he had turned on full power.

It was as if he had shouted to Moss:

" Race you to the line! "

Moss gave his car full throttle but he had rounded the corners more slowly. Fangio had a flying start on him. As they passed the end of the pits Fangio's nose went in front and for a moment everyone watching believed that Moss was to be robbed of the race that was rightly his.

In the nick of time Fangio realised that he had overdone things. He braked sharply and Moss went over the line a car's length in front to win his first Grand Prix.

At the end of the lap of honour Moss stopped in front of the little flight of steps that led from the track to the table where the trophy awaited him. Fangio ignored the invitation to follow and took his car away to its pit. To-day the spoils of the victor were for Moss.

179

They came first in the form of a smacking kiss from Mrs. Moss, the mother, and later in the shape of the *Daily Telegraph* and Mervyn O'Gorman Trophies. With his goggles and helmet off, the young driver wore on the part of his forehead which had been exposed to the fumes and swarf from the brake linings a distinct black " V."

Moss was handed the microphone and invited to say a few words to the crowd. He told them that Fangio was the greatest driver in the world and humbly thanked the Champion for letting him achieve his ambition to win the British Grand Prix.

This was indeed the first time in history that a British driver had won the race and the complete triumph of the four German cars was rendered more palatable by that fact.

The final seal was set on the proceedings by the playing of the German National Anthem. The crowd stood in decent silence. Maybe to some the tune recalled the words: " Deutschland, Deutschland über alles." Those who wanted were able to fix their minds on the alternative words which may be sung to the same tune: " Glorious things of thee are spoken."

OFFICIAL RESULTS

500 c.c. Race

Driver	Car	
1. Russell	Cooper-Norton	79·53 m.p.h.
2. Lewis-Evans	,,	
3. Fergusson	,,	
4. Leston	,,	

Sports Car Race

1. Salvadori	Aston-Martin	83·33 m.p.h.
2. Collins	,,	
3. Parnell	,,	
4. Walker	,,	

British Grand Prix

	Driver	Car		
1.	Moss	Mercedes-Benz	86·47 m.p.h.	90 laps
2.	Fangio	,,		90 ,,
3.	Kling	,,		90 ,,
4.	Taruffi	,,		89 ,,
5.	Musso	Maserati		89 ,,
6.	Hawthorn/Castellotti	Ferrari		87 ,,
7.	Sparken	Gordini		81 ,,
8.	Macklin	Maserati		79 ,,
9.	Wharton/Schell	Vanwall		72 ,,

Fastest lap: Moss 2 mins. 0·4 secs.   89·70 m.p.h.

CHAPTER SEVEN

FASTER! FASTER!

Italian Grand Prix. Monza. 11 September

STOP ANYWHERE on the northern outskirts of Milan and ask the first Italian you see the way to the *Autódromo di Monza*. His eyes will light up and with a chopping movement of his right hand he will urge you " *Avanti! Avanti!* " If motor racing has a native land, that land is surely Italy, and Monza is the hub of Italian racing. Standing about ten miles outside Milan it is very much the offspring of that city with its feverish bustle and relentless pursuit of progress. The near-million inhabitants of Milan have not forgotten that a hundred years ago their city was the capital of Italy and once was the seat of the Emperor of Rome. Proud of their modern efficiency they despise the more easy-going Romans and frequently clamour for the return of the capital to Milan. Business is their very lifeblood and most of the great commercial enterprises have their headquarters there. It is the Milanese who build the Alfa-Romeo cars, and it was the Automobile Club of Milan which conceived the idea of constructing the Autódromo.

Grands Prix had taken place in France for many years before the first Gran Premio d'Italia was organised in 1921. It took place on the Montechiari circuit, near Brescia—later to become the home of the Mille Miglia. The result was a resounding defeat of Italian men and machines. Goux in a

182

Ballot was first at 90·4 m.p.h., and Chassagne in a similar car was second. Even in those days success or failure in automobile engineering was a matter of national importance to Italians. Such a defeat was scarcely to be endured and there was talk of Italy withdrawing completely from motor racing. At this critical moment the *Automobile Club di Milano* hit on its brainwave of constructing a permanent circuit which would not only permit unrestricted organisation of races but also provide a testing ground for Italian cars. The site chosen was the Park of Monza Palace, seat of the Royal House of Savoy. The circuit was created in one hundred days. It consisted of a road circuit, linked to a high speed oval with slightly banked corners.

Something of the go-ahead atmosphere of Milan went into the building of the track and has hung about it ever since. At Monza speed is an idol worshipped by organisers and spectators, an idol to which drivers must pay sometimes unwilling obeisance. The watchword is " Faster! Faster! " Here are organised not only Grands Prix, but also sports car and motor-cycle races. The motor-cycle Grand Prix of the Nations had been held exactly a week before the 1955 Italian Grand Prix. The green and usually sunny park of Monza, with its wild fowl and its associations of a vanished monarchy, has probably seen more motor racing than any other European circuit. Perhaps that is why the death-roll amongst drivers is so high. Out of 50 drivers killed between 1923 and 1953 ten were killed at Monza. When the 1955 race was run the death of Ascari was still very much in people's minds.

The story of this classic event falls into two phases each represented by a rising graph of speeds. The result of the first Grand Prix run at Monza was a vindication of the *Automobile Club di Milano's* enterprise. Bordino on a Fiat was first at 83·69 m.p.h., and he was followed home by his team-mate Nazzaro. In 1923 this race was entitled The European Grand Prix. Fiat again took first and second places at the increased speed of 91·06. It was in this year that an unusual name appeared in the list of finishers in a European race. Jimmy Murphy in a Miller took third place. In 1924 Antonio Ascari led a 1–2–3–Alfa-Romeo victory at 98·76 m.p.h. By 1929 Achille Varzi was lapping the high-speed oval at 125 m.p.h. 1931, '32, '33 were the years of Alfa-Romeo supremacy and the honours lists were sprinkled with such great names as Nuvolari, Campari, Caracciola, Borzacchini and Fagioli.

Then in 1933 came Monza's fatal day. The Italian Grand Prix took place in the morning and was won by Fagioli at an average of 108·58 m.p.h. During this performance he raised the record for the combined circuit to 115·8 m.p.h. In the afternoon the Monza Grand Prix was run over the high-speed oval only, and a lap was soon registered by Guy Moll at 122 m.p.h. Drizzle and oil later made the track slippery and it was in these conditions that Campari and Borzacchini, racing neck and neck, touched hubs and spun to death. Not long afterwards Czaykowski, battling for the lead with Moll and Lehoux was blinded by flames from his burning engine, lost control and was burned to death in the wreckage of his car.

This black event put paid to Monza's high-speed oval, which disappeared beneath the dust and ashes, to rise Phœnix-like over twenty years later.

The years 1934 and 1938 saw faster cars winning at lower speeds on the all-road circuit. It was a chain of German victories, but the winning car was not always a Mercedes. In 1935 not one Mercedes-Benz finished. In 1936 they did not run at all. But when Mercedes fell by the wayside Auto-Union were always at hand and the Italian spectators chewed on gall and wormwood until in 1938 Nuvolari suddenly got the feel of the awkward rear-engined Auto-Union and gave them something to cheer about. His speed of 96·70 with this immensely powerful car was still 12 m.p.h. slower than the winning speed in 1933.

In 1949 the Italian Grand Prix returned to Monza. From then till now it has been dominated by the two great figures of post-war racing—Ascari and Fangio. In 1949 Ascari drove his Ferrari through to victory at 105·09 m.p.h. In 1951 Farina won at 109.63 m.p.h., but Ascari was second. In 1951 he was again first; his speed with the 4½ litre Ferrari was 115·45 m.p.h., and for the first time the 1933 figure was being exceeded. In 1952 the organisers adopted Formula Two and the speed went back to 109·8 m.p.h., but again Ascari was first, followed each time by the faithful Gonzalez.

1953 saw what was justly described by many as the Race of the Century and the emergence of a new car and a new driver. During the whole of this season Maserati had been gradually creeping up on the dominant Ferrari. By the Italian Grand Prix the cars were evenly matched and there was nothing to choose between the drivers. From the very first lap four cars shot out ahead of the rest of the field—Ascari and Farina on Ferraris and Fangio and Marimon on Maseratis. For forty-six laps these four were never separated by more than two seconds. The lead was constantly changing, often several times during the same lap. When they went past the grandstands at half distance each car was overlapping the one in front and in the next ten laps Ascari led for six, Farina for two and Fangio for two, whilst along the straight on the far side of the course it was Marimon who more than once got his nose in front. On the forty-sixth lap of the eighty Marimon had a pit stop but when he restarted he joined the fray as if nothing had happened. About the sixtieth lap the four leaders caught up Villoresi

185

and Hawthorn, and these two tacked on behind. For five laps the six cars stormed round in a tight bunch at 112 m.p.h. When they overtook slower cars they passed them some on one side and some on the other so that many a driver began to pay more attention to his mirrors than to the road ahead. At last Villoresi tapped his head and he and Hawthorn let the madmen draw away. Tails and noses were crumpled and at each corner the four leaders were slithering wide, playing frantically with their steering-wheels to keep the cars on the road. For the whole of seventy-nine laps it lasted and the cars stood up to it.

When they disappeared for the eightieth and last lap Ascari was in the lead and Fangio fourth, but it seemed that anything could happen. Everyone's eyes turned to the last bend leading into the final straight. A sudden cloud of dust arose and from it emerged two low red cars. They screamed past—Fangio followed by Farina. The hubbub of excited voices began. Where was Ascari? Where was Marimon? It was a long time before they appeared, walking up the road, Ascari not at all amused and Marimon with blood all over his jersey front. On the last bend Ascari had been leading. Whether he spun first or was shunted first by Marimon is not related, but certainly the two cars hit and went out of control. Farina, following very close behind and himself in no seraphic mood, was forced to swing wide to avoid them. Fangio, with his uncanny swiftness of reflex, was able to pounce on his opening and take the dicey Maserati through on the inside of the bend at undiminished speed. Afterwards, when they chaired and garlanded him, his eyes had a faraway look and his mind was still on that last corner.

1954 again brought drama and again it was the story of four cars and four drivers. This was not the neck and neck struggle of 1953 but a more reasoned and calculated game

186

of strategy. Ascari was once more mounted on Ferrari, having been lent for the occasion by the Lancia firm to whom he was now bound by contract; Fangio was number one for the new Mercedes-Benz team; Moss was using his own Maserati, now supported by the factory. These three drivers were on the front row of the starting grid. The race began as if the devil himself was out with his whip. On the second lap the race lap record was established and half the drivers recorded their fastest times. When sanity was restored it could be seen that Ascari had taken command, followed closely by Fangio. Moss was holding a watching brief. On lap 23 Fangio squeezed past the Italian Champion but Ascari almost immediately pushed his Ferrari in front again. Shortly before half distance grey-haired Villoresi came up from fourth place to make his bid for the lead, but in a very few laps his motor cracked up. On the forty-fifth lap Moss, who had passed Fangio, challenged Ascari and took the lead. In his efforts to snatch it back Ascari burst his engine. Now Moss, driving with complete calm and mastery of the situation, began to reap the rewards of his patient strategy. He had pulled out over 20 seconds ahead of Fangio and seemed to have the race in his pocket. But thirteen laps from the end his oil tank split. He had to push his car all the way from the Vedano Curve to the finish while the dogged Fangio sailed through to a victory he had not expected. When the chequered flag fell to him Fangio saluted the stationary Moss to show that he considered him the moral victor. The English driver had been sitting on the wheel of his car. Now he got up and to the wild applause of the crowd pushed his Maserati over the line to score tenth place.

The Italian Grand Prix has a way of producing drama, and this is largely due to its place on the calendar. Coming towards the end of the season but not at the very end it is often the point at which the World Championship is lost or won; and just as a race is decided in its closing stages, so the seal is set on the season by the result of this event. On the other hand Monza has more than once launched some new model or idea.

1955 had been, since Le Mans, a distorted season. There had been great gaps in the calendar instead of the French, German and Swiss Grands Prix. The continuance or otherwise of motor racing had become a political matter. Not only had a mass of spectators been killed but many more drivers than ever before had perished during this season. The Italian Minister of Transport, Armando Angellini, was outspoken in his animosity to racing. Shortly before the Grand Prix it became known that local authority had banned the Giro d'Italia and the historic Targa Florio, about to celebrate its fiftieth anniversary. The position of racing in Europe and particularly in Italy was at a critical stage.

It was in this atsmosphere that the Milan Automobile Club had been pushing on with their plans, conceived before Le Mans, to build a *pista per alte velocità*, which would allow race speeds higher than any achieved before. Their attitude, as bold as Charles Faroux's decision to allow the 24-hour race to continue, implied that danger does not lie in speed alone. Their new track was a resurrection in modernised form of the original Monza. To the road circuit of some $3\frac{1}{2}$ miles was now linked an oval track a little over $2\frac{1}{2}$ miles in circumference. It consisted of two long-banked curves— the Curva Nord and the Curva Sud—linked by two straight, flat sections of about 600 yards, one of which ran parallel with the road circuit in front of the pits and grandstands. The novelty consisted in the banked corners, each of which went on for over half a mile. Built of reinforced concrete set on pillars, they took the edge of the road up to a height

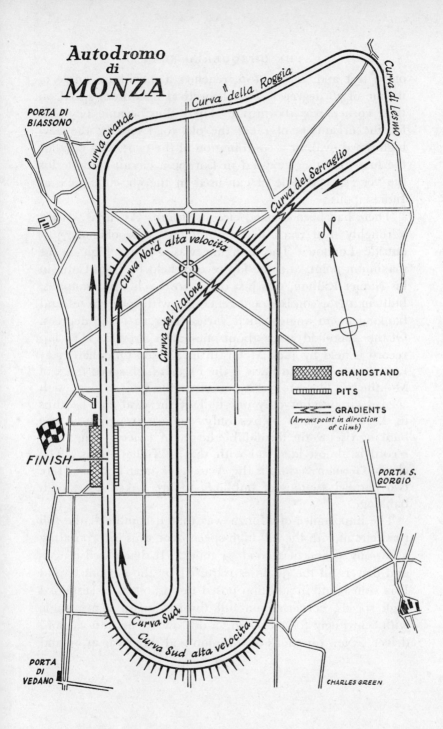

Autodromo di MONZA

PORTA DI BIASSONO

Curva Grande

Curva della Roggia

Curva di Lesmo

Curva del Serraglio

Curva Nord "alta velocita"

Curva del Vialone

N

GRANDSTAND

PITS

GRADIENTS
(Arrows point in direction of climb)

FINISH

PORTA S. GORGIO

Curva Sud

Curva Sud alta velocita

PORTA DI VEDANO

CHARLES GREEN

of 19 feet and, at the top, reached a maximum angle of incline of 38 degrees. The theoretical maximum speed on these corners was 160 m.p.h. There thus became available for the organisers of races the old road circuit, the new high-speed oval, or a combination of the two; and now for the first time there existed in Europe a circuit suitable for the very special type of car used in the 500-mile race at Indianapolis.

There had been banked circuits before. As early as 1907 a roughly oval track had been built at Brooklands, just outside London. The banking was 25 feet high at its maximum point, and the lap record, held by John Cobb in his Napier Railton, was just over 140 m.p.h. Indianapolis, built in 1910, consists of a rectangle with four curves and banking at an angle which varies from 16 to 36 degrees. Of the 4,000-odd yards about one-half is straight. The lap record is held by Jack McGrath in a 4,500 Offenhauser at 143 m.p.h. Close to Paris is the French high-speed track of Montlhéry; like Monza it combines the banked oval with a road circuit, but only one-half of the oval can be thus used. Of its 3,000 metres only 350 are straight and the banking rises to the formidable height of 32 feet. The track record is almost identical with that of Indianapolis. The closest German version is the Avus track near Berlin. Here two parallel sections of public road are linked by a high banking.

The importance of Monza was that it combined the full road circuit with the full high-speed oval, thus incorporating a flat-out section of a good 2½ miles. It demanded of cars and drivers all the qualities required by the normal Grand Prix course and in addition posed the problems of sustained high speeds, cornering on full throttle at an acute angle with centrifugal force exerting a downward pull on car and driver. New questions of adhesion and tyre wear arose and drivers were faced with the necessity of mastering a completely new technique.

The work of construction, which had consumed 750,000 man hours and involved moving 110,000 cubic metres of earth, was completed a few weeks before the date fixed for the Italian Grand Prix. As soon as it was available the interested manufacturers turned their cars and drivers loose on it. They wanted to waste no time in finding out how their men and machines were going to stand up to the new conditions. Alarmist reports were soon circulating to the effect that the drivers had said the new track was too dangerous; that Fangio had stated he would not race unless he was strapped in with a safety belt. In fact there were tremendous bumps where the sections of concrete joined, but they were pared down and soon things began to happen. Fangio, Farina and Moss lapped the combined circuits at about 138 m.p.h. Public interest in the forthcoming race was not diminished by the news of these speeds nor the suggestion that they involved hideous risks.

The Grand Prix circus reassembled at Monza after almost two months of marking time. Meanwhile, an important development had taken place. Lancia had sportingly handed over to Ferrari their complete set of Grand Prix cars and the great F.I.A.T. concern had come across with substantial monetary assistance to help keep the Italian colours flying. Ferrari had therefore entered six cars—three Lancias and three Ferraris. Maserati were known to be preparing a new, more streamlined car with petrol tanks slung, Lancia-like, between the wheels, and Gordini was at last ready with a new streamlined model of completely new conception. The Vanwalls were going to have another try and the two private Maseratis from England, Horace Gould's and Stirling Moss's. The latter, the very car which so nearly won the race in 1954, was this time to be piloted by John Fitch, and had been repainted in the American colours of silver and blue for the occasion. Its two gallant mechanics had adapted it to the needs of four different drivers in as many races, and kept it going with the devotion of pedigree horse trainers.

As for drivers, Moss was still with Mercedes, Hawthorn had returned definitely to Ferrari and—a significant augur for the future—Collins was newly signed up to drive for Maserati. So there was a British driver in each of the hot teams. It would be interesting to pick international racing teams on the driver basis. Italy might decide that the veterans Farina and Villoresi had lost their relish for a needle match, though she could certainly not exclude old man Taruffi. Castellotti is an automatic choice, perhaps the most dashing and colourful figure in motor racing to-day. Musso, by virtue of his experience and steadiness must be preferred to the brilliant but impetuous Perdisa. France can produce Behra and Trintignant, and for third man would perhaps prefer Simon to Manzon. The Argentine offers formidable possibilities. Their team, led by Fangio, would include the precision driver Mieres, and now that Gonzalez has retired from the scene, the startling newcomer Menditeguy. Germany, though she produces the cars, does not seem to have the men and Kling and Hermann would have to conduct talent-spotting contests to find their supporter. Britain's team would be Messrs. Moss, Hawthorn, and Collins. Oh, that we could see them all together!

During the first of the two official days of practice Farina suffered an experience almost as startling for the other entrants as for himself. Whistling round the new banking like a conker on the end of a string his Lancia threw a tread from one of its tyres at something like 160 m.p.h. He spun twice, thumped the yellow, sprung safety wall lining the

ITALIAN GRAND PRIX

ENTRY LIST

Driver					Car
Farina	..	..	..	..	Lancia
Castellotti	..	..	..	..	Lancia
Hawthorn	..	..	..	..	Ferrari
Trintignant	..	..	..	..	Ferrari
Villoresi	..	..	..	..	Lancia
Maglioli	..	..	..	..	Ferrari
Taruffi	..	..	..	..	Mercedes
Moss	..	..	..	..	Mercedes
Fangio	..	..	..	..	Mercedes
Kling	..	..	..	..	Mercedes
Da Silva Ramos	..	..	..	..	Gordini
Manzon	..	..	..	..	Gordini
Pollet	..	..	..	..	Gordini
Mieres	..	..	..	..	Maserati
Musso	..	..	..	..	Maserati
Collins	..	..	..	..	Maserati
Menditeguy	..	..	..	..	Maserati
Behra	..	..	..	..	Maserati
Gould	..	..	..	..	Maserati
Fitch	..	..	..	..	Maserati
Schell	..	..	..	..	Vanwall
Wharton	..	..	..	..	Vanwall
Arzani	..	..	..	..	Piotti

outside edge of the track and came to rest right side up. His comment:

"An interesting experiment, but what would have happened had half a dozen other cars been following me?"

Villoresi was known to be no lover of the new track, least of all when required to circulate it in the unhappily tyred Lancia. Rumour stated that he had flatly refused to compete unless the old course was used. As usual, Fangio recorded the best official time of 2 minutes 46 8/10 seconds. Moss was as yet unable to practice in his own car. It was still being draped in a one-piece Dior-like streamlined creation at the factory. It arrived on Saturday aboard the 115 m.p.h. lorry which Daimler-Benz used for transporting race-cars.

On Saturday the Milanese skies opened and torrential rain fell all morning. The teams were assembled to test the effects of rain on the track and whilst they paddled round trailing clouds of spray the rain trickled down the saucer bankings and formed deep ponds on the inside of the new corners. Any driver who took his hands off the wheel on the banking would soon have established a handsome water speed record. The weather cleared up at midday. Moss had at last got his car. He took it out and after a few cautionary laps established second best time, 1½ seconds slower than Fangio. Kling had lapped in 2 minutes 48 3/10 seconds and so three Mercedes had taken the three places on the front row of the starting grid. The fastest Italian was Castellotti on his Lancia, three seconds a lap slower than Fangio.

Certain differences of opinion were apparent about the correct technique on the new curves. Taruffi believed that the best method was to go round all the way near the very top. Castellotti's method was similar, though his line was a little lower. Collins and the official Maserati team were convinced that the one and only way was to enter the corner

194

well to the outside, swing down slightly on the way round
and then cross to the extreme outside on the exit. Moss
reckoned that it was a good thing to keep low from start to
finish. He placed his wheels just above the yellow line
painted to mark the centre and avoided swinging too wide
either on the entry or the exit. He described the banking
as being neither like an ordinary straight nor an ordinary
corner. Though it was possible to go round on full throttle
there was an uneasy, twitching movement, and the tendency
of the car was to steer down to the bottom of the banking.

I was lucky to be able to form an impression of the course
at a fair speed. Starting from in front of the grandstand you
first embark on the road circuit. The Curva Grande is a
real test of driving skill, being one of those fast bends which
can be taken almost flat out. The ensuing Curva della
Roggia is noticeable only at the very highest speeds, but the
double curves of Lesmo are very sharp and treacherous. The
racers take these corners at between 80 and 90 m.p.h. in
third. Then comes a downhill swoop, which carries the
road slap underneath the fantastic banking of the oval. The
highest speeds can be reached here so that the Curva del
Vialone, a flat-out bend with a twitchy bump at the top,
becomes a definite problem. Here Ascari was killed.
Maximum speed can be reached down the back straight
before the new Curvetta Sud, a bend very reminiscent of
Becher's Bend at Aintree. The surface here is very new
black tarmac and it holds the wet after rain. Tight at the
beginning, the curve gradually opens out so that power can
be turned on before the straight is reached. Now you run
parallel to the start and finish straight and past the front
of the pits. The apparently vertical wall of the banking
moves towards you with appalling suddenness even at such
a moderate speed as 120 m.p.h. The first impressions on
being committed to a corner at undiminished speed are

novel. As the car heels abruptly to an acute angle two fierce
bumps threaten to send you either through the floor or the
roof. You feel like a roulette ball spun round the inside of
a wheel which is revolving in the opposite direction. Ahead
stretches the visible quadrant of banked cineramic concrete,
the sky is all to hell and below the side window is an ugly
brown pond and streaking trees. There is nothing to give
a true indication of speed. The curve apparently goes on
for ever and ever; you've given up hope of getting out of
this wall of death when the car comes on to an even keel
and the black surface of the straight section sucks you
towards it. In a few seconds the banking at the other end
scoops you up with sinister eagerness and you have to go
through the whole business all over again. When you steam
off the banking for the second time the double roadway is
ahead of you, leading back to the chequered line in front
of the grandstand where the race starts and finishes. Even
one tour produces mixed feelings, yet on Race Day the
competitors are called upon to go round this circuit fifty
times.

Skies were grey on Sunday morning but by 10.30 the sun
was trying to come through. Italian enthusiasts are not so
prepared to brave the elements as their British counterparts,
but as the skies lightened the waverers decided to go out
to Monza. The new circuit was a draw, and after all,
the President of the Republic was going to be there to
open it.

Already at 9.30 saloon cars were battering round the road
circuit. The curtain raiser for the Grand Prix was the Coppa
Inter Europa. It was run in two heats, won respectively
by Von Hanstein's Porsche and Guarducci's 8 V Zagato
Fiat.

The production cars were flagged in at 12.30 and as their
somewhat muffled concert of sound died away the crisper,

naked noises from the paddock indicated that preparations were already intensifying for the 26th *Gran Premio d'Italia* due to begin at 3.0 p.m.

Spectators from the public enclosures spread out their picnics under the trees of the Royal Park. Holders of grandstand tickets repaired to the vast restaurant with its glass front which runs along the whole ground-floor length of the stand. Plates of lobster and chicken were born to the pits rented by non-competitors at £700 a time. Quite a lot of money was on the move that afternoon. Perhaps £10,000 had been laid out in starting money by the organisers. Incalculable expense had been incurred in the research and construction of the cars. Many of the entrants had been paid large sums in return for contracts with oil companies and accessory manufacturers. The £3,000 prize money was a mere flea-bite. The prestige effect of victory was what Germany and Italy were after. There is no way of calculating to what extent the demonstration given by Mercedes-Benz during 1955 has affected the sales of these cars in particular, and of all German-made articles in general. If people in future years express astonishment at the rise in German exports let the motor races of 1955 not be forgotten.

As the last hours before this last Grand Prix went by, the familiar sights and scenes of the paddock were punctuated by some unusual features. Red, blue, silver and green cars; mechanics in white, blue or yellow overalls; the drivers with their sleek, private cars and well-turned girl friends; autograph hunters; camera men and reporters. Maglioli sat in his Ford Thunderbird with a plaid-trousered lady; Neubauer was ensconced at a table behind one of his lorries, holding a council of war with Fangio, Moss, Kling and Taruffi. This was to be the last race of the German Grand Prix team; news of their withdrawal the following season had been confirmed.

Ferrari had decided that the Mercedes idea of roping off their area was a good one. They had brought a piece of their own, but it was not long enough and for some minutes an Italian mechanic stood disconsolately holding the spare end. Somehow it seemed to sum up the whole difference between the German team and their rivals. Moss, wanting a private word with his lady friend, walked her rapidly up and down the paddock as if they were both after a train. The reason soon was clear. When he came to rest he was immediately surrounded by autographers and questioners.

Standing in the corner of the paddock was a clerical figure in skull cap and purple flowing cloak. He was the Archpriest of Monza awaiting the arrival of the Cardinal of Milan amongst petrol tenders and transport lorries.

At 1.40 the first Mercedes engine started and continued to run with a steady roar. The news began to circulate that Lancia had withdrawn from the race. They had been unable to solve their tyre troubles. Contracts prevented them from receiving help from any of the rival teams. Mercedes had intimated that if the Lancias ran they would withdraw. Farina and Villoresi accepted the decision but Castellotti begged and badgered to be allowed to drive a car on his own account as he had done at Spa. At last they agreed to let him drive in the practice Ferrari, the hack car known as The Mule which is belaboured in turn by every driver. Training consistently in Lancias, Castellotti had never even tried his mount on the new course, but he went away as happy as a sandboy.

The President was due at three o'clock. Shortly before that the gates from the paddock were opened and the cars were pushed out in file, each driver walking beside his own. At the head came dark young Castellotti in sky-blue trousers and yellow jersey, leading his Mule. The grandstand rose to him. The cars were parked in their positions on the starting grid. The drivers lined up on the roadway between grandstand and pit, opposite the gateway through which the President would arrive. On the stands and at the gates appeared members of the President's Private Guard, the Corazieri; men six and a half foot high with brass helmets, plumes, breastplates and swords. The last remnant of royalty and panache, they accompany the Head of the State whenever he goes about his lawful occasions. A red and cream 3 litre open sports Maserati stood waiting on the roadway by the gate.

Prompt at three the sun came out. Still no sign of Signor Gronchi. Shortly afterwards a posse of carabinieri outriders and a storm of ironic cheers and whistles heralded the arrival of the President. No sooner had he alighted from his car than he was buttonholed by the President of the *Automobile Club di Milano* who made a lengthy speech in praise of motor racing. The significance of the President's decision to approve with his presence this fastest ever race was not to be lost. The speech went on and on.[1] A lone Grand Prix engine interjected its fierce, snarling comment from the starting grid. The drivers of seven nations—Argentine, Britain, France, Germany, Italy, Switzerland, United States, sat like a row of starlings on the safety wall. This delay extended and intensified the usual tension they suffered before a race, especially heightened before this one. Fangio, calmest of them all, sat on the roadway back to back with another driver in the massive shadow of his team manager, Neubauer. The crowd grew restive and the slow clap began.

At last the speech ended. Whistles and groans greeted the belated appearance of the President, followed by no less

---

[1] Perhaps the time was well spent, for in due course the Targa Florio was run as planned.

a dignitary than the Pope's Private Secretary, Cardinal Montoni of Milan, clad in purple cloak and mitre and lace apron. Drivers were presented and the twin representatives of temporal and spiritual power took their places in waiting cars, Gronchi in the sports Maserati and the Cardinal with retinue in a more sober Alfa-Romeo. When his tour of the road circuit ended the President was seen to urge his driver on; to the cheers of the crowd the Head of the State was swung on to the banking of the speed oval at 120 m.p.h. Meanwhile, the Cardinal, proceeding at a more reasonable gait, had stopped at the place where Ascari was killed in order to give his blessing.

Tours of honour completed, the real business of the day could now begin, some thirty-five minutes after time. Official brows were furrowed. If the race ran slower than expected or dark clouds gathered, then the last laps might be run in failing light and that could spell disaster. As the President took his seat in the *Tribune d'Honneur* eyes turned to the small compact bunch of cars on the broad roadway. Drivers were in their seats, engines were running and the starter was already on his rostrum. The shouting and gesticulating ceased; the attention of 150,000 knowledgeable, though wildly excited spectators, was concentrated on the twenty cars, and the track round which they would soon be hurtling.

Less than a minute to go.

This 1955 Italian Grand Prix was not characterised by any sensational struggle for the lead, but it was enlivened by a series of keen tussles for the other places and by a series of dramatic mechanical incidents. It seems best to try and convey some idea of it by reproducing the original form in which it was recorded by one observer at Lesmo Corner and another at the grandstands. From this latter vantage point the cars could be seen at three points on each lap.

First when they went along the straight in front of the stands, secondly as they passed their pits half-way round the course, and thirdly as they proceeded down the back straight of the road circuit. Monza in fact had become the best course for seeing every phase of the race, for by looking to the right the watcher from the top of the stands could see the cars coming out of the normal south curve and also leaving the banked part of the course. Through two distant gaps in the trees they could be seen for an instant as they flashed round the North or South curves.

Lap 1

KLING	**MOSS**	**FANGIO**
Mercedes	Mercedes	Mercedes
	CASTELLOTTI	
	Ferrari	
MIERES		**BEHRA**
Maserati		Maserati
MUSSO	**TARUFFI**	
Maserati	Mercedes	
SCHELL	**MAGLIOLI**	**COLLINS**
Vanwall	Ferrari	Maserati
TRINTIGNANT	**HAWTHORN**	
Ferrari	Ferrari	
DA SILVA RAMOS	**WHARTON**	**MENDITEGUY**
Gordini	Vanwall	Maserati
FITCH	**POLLET**	
Maserati	Gordini	
LUCAS	**GOULD**	
Gordini	Maserati	

At the fall of the flag Moss makes a brilliantly smooth getaway and shoots into the lead, followed closely by Kling. Fangio makes a slower start than usual and is third as the mass of roaring, smoking cars disappears. As the field bursts unexpectedly into the view of the crowds waiting at

Lesmo the order is Moss, Kling, Fangio, Taruffi with Castellotti and Hawthorn on their heels. As they tear down the back straight a red car is seen to be up amongst the Mercedes. A whole bunch emerge from the Curvetta Sud, headed by three silver cars. The field rush past the pits in the order: Moss, Fangio, Taruffi, Castellotti, Kling, Hawthorn, Mieres, Maglioli, Collins, Behra, Gould, Pollet, Schell, Trintignant, Musso, da Silva Ramos, Menditeguy, Lucas; the amazing thing is that Castellotti, who might have been expected to take a little time finding out how his car behaves on this strange circuit, is already right up among the German machines. One driver has pulled in to his pit. It is Wharton on the British green Vanwall. Even before it has completed one lap the car is retired with transmission trouble.

Lap 2

As the nineteen cars, already well strung out after only six miles, swing off the banking of the South Curve to complete their first lap it is seen that the order has changed. Fangio has taken the lead from Moss; Taruffi is third and Kling has passed Castellotti into fourth place. Mieres has squeezed his Maserati in front of Hawthorn's Ferrari. The new Gordini, a pretty, streamlined blue car, piloted by the Swiss Lucas in place of Manzon, is last.

Lap 3

The first seven cars are the same, but Collins has come up to eighth position and Gould in his private Maserati is well placed at twelfth. Before he reaches Lesmo he has taken his car past Maglioli in an official Ferrari. Then comes a tight bunch of cars, scrapping fiercely among themselves— Schell, Menditeguy, Trintigant, Pollet, da Silva. Across the fields on the back straight Moss can be seen closing up to less than a car's length from Fangio as they slow for the Curvetta Sud. The race average has already risen to 206·6 k.p.h., equal to about 130 m.p.h.

Lap 4

Seven and a half minutes have gone by and the first cars have already travelled 18 miles. The order of the leaders remains unchanged, but the gaps are visibly widening. Castellotti is driving for all he is worth, taking Lesmo at the limit and raising dust as he slithers off the edge of the road. Musso, gaining ground steadily, has passed Behra and now comes up to take eighth place from Collins.

Lap 5

Superior power is telling now and the Mercedes are inexorably drawing ahead. Fangio and Moss in the fully streamlined cars lead Kling and Taruffi in the more conventional models with their exposed wheels. Try as he may Castellotti has lost 200 yards to the last of the German cars. Menditeguy slithers in to his pit and after a brief halt is away again. The surviving Vanwall seems to be about on a par with the Gordinis, now increased to 2½ litres capacity. Hawthorn repasses Mieres, and Behra again thrusts the new sleek Maserati in front of Musso's older model. Fangio has set the official lap record at 2 minutes 51 1/10 seconds or about 131·5 m.p.h.

Lap 7

Hawthorn's car appears to be slowing. Musso, having passed him, overtakes Mieres also and sets off after Castellotti. Gould is in tenth position, Schell twelfth. Collins, who has been pointing with his thumb at the tail of his car, stops at his pit. The four Mercedes are already lapping Menditeguy, who since his pit stop is last.

Lap 8

Only 200 yards cover the four leading Mercedes. There is so little between them that Kling, in passing Taruffi to take his place in the proper team order, has achieved a new lap record at 2 minutes 50 4/10 seconds. Schell comes into his pit making signals towards his right rear axle. A de Dion tube is broken and the second Vanwall retires. He is not the only one making signals. Both Collins and Gould are pointing ominous thumbs at their tails. The very low Maseratis are scraping their bottoms on the bumps of the new banking and removing a sixteenth of an inch each time.

Lap 10

In front of the pits Kling passes Moss to occupy second place for a spell. It is beginning to look as if the Mercedes are going to give an even more convincing display of dominance than at Aintree. No one is challenging them here. There is now an appreciable gap before Castellotti appears. He is hollering round the banking as high as he can go and on the road corners his elbows are working to control the beginning of slides in a manner that is reminiscent of his master Ascari when he was really trying. The crowd have taken him to their hearts and urge him to even greater efforts. The long-suffering Mule, rather like the ugly duckling, is showing its rather prissy team-mates that it is as good as them any day and only needs someone who understands it.

Lap 11

Trintignant's turn to call briefly at his pit. Hawthorn's car checks as he passes the same point. He almost looks as if he's missed a gear.

Lap 12

A Gordini, $1\frac{1}{2}$ laps behind the leading Mercedes, comes off the banking just as they emerge from the Curvetta Sud. Not till they have covered 400 yards are the Mercedes able to reach its speed. This gives some idea of how the banked corners are allowing much greater velocities along the straight in front of the stands.

Lap 13

The order is still:

1. Fangio	6. Musso
2. Moss	7. Mieres
3. Kling	8. Behra
4. Taruffi	9. Hawthorn
5. Castellotti	

Only two seconds separate Moss and Fangio. The former seems as relaxed and comfortable as ever. Taruffi on the other hand is crouched over his wheel, seeming to urge his car on. Musso is closing steadily on Castellotti, whose driving becomes more and more dramatic as he fights to stave off the challenge.

Lap 16

In front of the stands Musso draws level with Castellotti, passes him. By Lesmo, Castellotti is in front again, but before the pair race past the pits Musso holds an advantage of 100 yards.

Lap 17

The race average has risen to 208 k.p.h. and Fangio and Moss have settled down to their usual tandem act. At Lesmo they are taking the same line but on the following fast left-hand swerve Moss constantly pulls out as if to pass Fangio,

205

yet never does. On each lap they take their wheels over the identical spot with hairsbreadth accuracy. They are making these amazing averages of over 130 m.p.h. look as easy as bicycle riding.

Lap 19

The stands rise as Musso and Castellotti come past wheel to wheel, neither of them prepared to yield an inch. A few minutes later when the leading Mercedes come snaking out of the Curvetta Sud it is seen that Moss is breaking off to pull into his pit. Even before the car stops he is pointing to the windshield. Having motored on Fangio's tail for some thousand miles odd during 1955 races he now pays the penalty. The windshield is shattered by a piece of the new concrete thrown up from Fangio's tyres, and the buffeting of a 180-mile-an-hour gale is too much to withstand. He jumps out and as mechanics start to replace the windshield he takes a long pull at the bottle. As the three other Mercedes stream past on the parallel road he climbs into the seat again and sets off, nearly two minutes in arrears.

Laps 20, 21 and 22

The race has now two very interesting features. The first is the duel between Castellotti and Musso which has been going on for five laps. Passing the grandstands Castellotti is apparently trying to unnerve Musso by swerving to and fro within inches of his rear tyres. He is in front of the Maserati at Lesmo and again at the pits, but after the tour round the oval it is Musso who is suddenly 200 yards ahead. Meanwhile Moss has set out to make up for lost time. It is easy to make a comparison between his speed and Fangio for as the Champion comes out of the Curvetta Sud Moss is just storming off the banking. After 3 laps it is apparent that Moss has gained about 500 yards though he is still

FASTER FASTER

about a minute and four seconds behind him on the road.
It is no surprise when the announcement comes that he has
broken the lap record and set a new time of 2 minutes
46 2/10 seconds, a speed of 134 m.p.h. His line at Lesmo is
as immaculate as ever, no slithering, no sawing of the
elbows. Only on the twenty-fifth lap does a squeak from
his tyres indicate that for once Moss is driving at the limit.

For a few minutes the three British drivers, Moss,
Hawthorn and Collins are in line ahead, but almost at once
Collins pulls in to his pit and retires.

Lap 26

1. Fangio	6. Behra
2. Kling	7. Moss
3. Taruffi	8. Hawthorn
4. Musso	9. Maglioli
5. Castellotti	10. Pollet

The race average is 208·5 k.p.h., equalling just about
130 m.p.h.

Lap 27

Cars are beginning to come in for tyre changes and fuel
replenishment. Gould is in and away but as he comes
round again he is still pointing ominously at his stern. Fitch,
in Moss's car, is flagged in by Alf Francis and after a smooth
tyre change and refill is off again with a healthy sounding
exhaust note. But this car which in 1954 was fast enough
to lead the field is now at the tail end, such is the progress
achieved in one year. Musso charges in to change his
rear wheels and collect a new pair of goggles. When he
re-starts his car takes umbrage and he disappears at a snail's
pace.

Lap 28

In eight laps Moss, by a feat of superb driving has won back a whole minute. Spectators realise that although team discipline will not allow him to win, Moss may provide them with the spectacle of a classic drive as he hauls his way back to Fangio's tail before the end of the race.

Lap 29

For a moment Taruffi shows in front of Kling. The Italian crowd is delighted but when Taruffi lets the German pass him again they shake their fingers at him admonishingly.

Lap 30

It is suddenly apparent that Moss is overdue. He passes Lesmo slowing down and waving the other cars past. The crowd gives the popular British driver a round of sympathetic applause. He coasts down the hill and stops at the Curva del Vialone from which there's only a short walk back to the pits. Once again engine trouble has struck at the Mercedes.

Lap 32

Musso is in trouble. For the third time in as many laps he calls at his pit. Fangio laps Hawthorn.

Lap 33

As Kling comes off the banking behind Fangio and Taruffi he is rapidly losing speed. In front of the stands he almost comes to a standstill and casts a longing glance at his pit as if he would like to break all the regulations and cross the parallel road to reach it. He quickly looks behind and with the last dregs of impetus pulls the Mercedes across the road on to the grass verge in front of the stands. He delves about in the gear box, hunting for a gear that will engage, then gives it up and switches off. He climbs out of the car, clambers over the railings and disappears through the subway towards the pits. That's two Mercedes out and there are 18 laps to go. Castellotti's Mule looks ready to gallop round the world and back again.

Meanwhile both Musso and Gould have called at their pits yet again and decided to call it a day.

Lap 34

Hawthorn, passed by Fangio and Taruffi some two laps ago, has found new life in his Ferrari. On the back straight he actually leads Taruffi for a moment and passes the pits in the Italian's slipstream, his red nose an inch away from the silver tail.

Lap 37

The order is:

1. Fangio	6. Mieres
2. Taruffi	7. Maglioli
3. Castellotti	8. Trintignant
3. Behra	9. Fitch
5. Hawthorn	

Only these nine cars are left in the race and the overall average has dropped to 207·9 k.p.h. Hawthorn stops to refuel and is away again in 36 seconds.

Lap 38

Hawthorn stops at his pit again. The movements of his hand indicate that the handling of his car makes it unmanageable. His pit staff urge him on and he accelerates away, shaking his head.

Lap 39

Hawthorn appears round the Curvetta Sud, motoring very slowly. This time he has taken his helmet off to show that there is no question of going on, and his blond head glints in the light. So now all the British cars and all the British drivers are out of the race. Mieres also is in trouble and making frequent visits to his pit.

Lap 40

The contest is entering its closing stages. The leading Mercedes continue to circulate with clockwork regularity, Taruffi now playing the role of Fangio's shadow. It is difficult to realise that what one is witnessing is a majestically display of controlled speed. The two silver cars pass the grandstands; 1 minute and 15 seconds later they appear on the back straight; after 1 minute 50 seconds they have rounded the Curvetta Sud and go past the pits; exactly 1 minute later they complete the lap and flash over the black and white chequered strip painted on the roadway. The crowd now realises that Castellotti can never catch them up. He is almost a minute behind. But a keen struggle is developing for third place. Behra, who has driven with polished restraint, is now putting on the pressure and closing on Castellotti. He in his turn is being harried by Menditeguy. Since the fifteenth lap this newcomer from the Argentine has been going round in close company with Behra. Their duel has lasted for 30 laps and although in fact a lap ahead the French champion just has not been able to shake his pursuer off.

Laps 45–50.

Behra in challenging Castellotti has at last drawn away from Menditeguy. Signals from the Ferrari pit warn Castellotti of the Maserati threat. He speeds up and as the distance between the two cars increases to 24 seconds the struggle seems finally decided in favour of Castellotti. The Mule has been trailing a haze of blue smoke behind it on the straight, but it's nothing to the thick cloud which follows Behra when he appears, just as Fangio and Taruffi are about to start their last lap. He drags the Maserati away in an attempt to get it round the course once more so as to qualify as a finisher, but with a broken piston rattling about he's hardly doing 50 m.p.h.

Mesdames Fangio and Taruffi are brought to the finishing-line to greet the triumphant return of their husbands with bouquets and kisses. As the two leaders pass the pits, Taruffi, with a surge of Roman enthusiasm, treads heavily on the gas and goes past Fangio. The crowd roars but Taruffi waves reassuringly and drops back obediently to second place. Fangio continues with complete calm; nobody but he knows what average speeds he could have set up with that car on this track had he really been pushed. Say, 140 m.p.h.?

The cars appear for the last time, the chequered flag flutters. Fangio has won for the third year running and set the seal on a year of brilliant successes for Mercedes-Benz. The crowd is overjoyed to see their old favourite Taruffi second and their new favourite Castellotti third.

Menditeguy romps past to complete his forty-ninth lap and the chequered flag prevents him from continuing his pursuit of Behra, now somewhere out in the hinterland coaxing the smoking Maserati towards the finish. At last he appears, travelling at about 20 m.p.h., and crosses the line, some four minutes after the winners, to take fourth place. Fangio, Taruffi and Castellotti complete their lap of honour. The crowds break through the police cordon to chair Fangio and Taruffi and to overwhelm Castellotti with hugs and kisses.

OFFICIAL RESULTS

1. Fangio	Mercedes	2 hrs. 25 mins.	4 4/10 secs.
		206·791 k.p.h.	
2. Taruffi	Mercedes	2 hrs. 25 mins.	5 1/10 secs.
3. Castellotti	Ferrari	2 hrs. 25 mins.	50 6/10 secs.
4. Behra	Maserati	2 hrs. 29 mins.	01 1/10 secs.
5. Menditeguy	Maserati	49 laps	
6. Maglioli	Ferrari	49 ,,	
7. Mieres	Maserati	48 ,,	
8. Trintignant	Ferrari	47 ,,	
9. Fitch	Maserati	46 ,,	

Fastest lap: Moss 2 minutes 46 9/10 seconds
215·7 k.p.h. (137 m.p.h.)

*　　*　　*

The European season ended with two events in the Sports Car Championship, the Ulster Tourist Trophy and the Sicilian Targa Florio. Moss was victorious in both, partnered in turn by Fitch and Collins. In the Tourist Trophy three British drivers were killed and the three German cars took the first three places. In the Targa Florio they were placed first, second and fourth.

Never before has there been a combination of cars and drivers which gave so certain a promise of victory as Fangio and Moss mounted on Mercedes-Benz. These manufacturers entered for thirteen races in 1955 with the following results:

Argentine Grand Prix:	1st. Fangio
Buenos Aires Grand Prix:	1st. Fangio, 2nd. Moss
Mille Miglia:	1st. Moss, 2nd. Fangio
Eiffelrenen:	1st. Fangio, 2nd. Moss
Monaco Grand Prix:	No score

Netherlands Grand Prix:	1st. Fangio, 2nd. Moss
Belgian Grand Prix:	1st. Fangio, 2nd. Moss
Le Mans	Fangio/Moss withdrawn when in the lead
British Grand Prix:	1st. Moss, 2nd. Fangio, 3rd. Kling, 4th. Taruffi
Swedish Grand Prix:	1st. Fangio, 2nd. Moss
Italian Grand Prix:	1st. Fangio, 2nd. Taruffi
Tourist Trophy:	1st. Moss, 2nd. Fangio, 3rd. Von Trips
Targa Florio:	1st. Moss/Collins, 2nd. Fangio/Kling, 4th. Titterington/Fitch

Need it be added that the Championship was won by Juan Fangio, the fastest motorist the world has seen?

If Germany demonstrated the superiority of her machines, it was Britain which proved that she is the richest source of racing drivers. Moss was second in the World Championship for Grand Prix drivers and absolute Champion in Sports Cars. Of the six Sports Car Championship races five were won by British drivers.

Sebring 12-hour race:	Hawthorn (with Walters)
Mille Miglia:	Moss
Le Mans:	Hawthorn and Bueb
Tourist Trophy:	Moss (with Fitch)
Targa Florio:	Moss and Collins

Never before has this country enjoyed such superiority in racing manpower. For whom will Moss, Hawthorn, Collins and Titterington be driving in 1956 Grands Prix? Now that Mercedes-Benz have announced their definite retirement there will be no lack of offers from other Continental firms. Is it too much to hope that there will be a British enterprise worthy of their merit? Dare we predict that the result of that appendix to the European Calendar, the Syracuse Grand Prix, is a portent? It was won by a lone British driver in a lone British car—Brooks at the wheel of a Connaught.

*   *   *

Since my first chapter was written the spotlight of publicity has been directed on the Dangers of Motor Racing. At the end of a book about some of the events of 1955, the most tragic year in the history of racing, it is perhaps appropriate to give some consideration to this question.

George Monkhouse's book, *Grand Prix Racing*, contains some very interesting tables. The results of over 1,000 European races from 1898 to 1952 are listed. Another table shows that during the same period of fifty-four years fifty-nine drivers competing in these events were killed, nineteen of them during practice. It would seem reasonable to allow an average distance of three hundred miles for each race and an average entry of twenty. This means that on a very rough calculation one driver was killed for every hundred-thousand miles covered by cars in practice and races at an average of a little over one every year.

There have been three occasions when casualties to spectators were high: in the 1903 Paris-Madrid race ten were killed at various points along the route; in 1936 a car competing in the Ulster T.T. crashed on to the pavement at Newtonards and eight people died; in 1938 a Mille Miglia competitor crashed at Bologna and the death-roll was twenty.

Just lately, however, there has been an abrupt increase. The number of spectator casualties was suddenly tripled by the Le Mans accident with its death-roll of eighty-three. In European races this year nine drivers were killed, three of them in the Ulster T.T.

The following list was drawn up from reports in motoring

journals. The Fédération Internationale de l'Automobile, although it is the body which is supposed to control motor racing, did not possess a record of fatal accidents.

Drivers killed during 1955

Name	Circumstances	Type of car
Alberto Ascari	Unofficial practice, Monza	Ferrari sports
Pierre Levegh	24-hour race, Le Mans	Mercedes sports
Don Beauman	Leinster Trophy, Ireland	Connaught sports
Piero Valenzano	Dolomite Cup, Italy	Maserati sports
Mike Keen	9-hour race, Goodwood	Cooper-Bristol sports
R. Sleeman	Bouley Bay Hill Climb	Cooper supercharged
Jim Mayers	Tourist Trophy, Ulster	Cooper-Climax sports
Bill Smith	,, ,, ,,	Connaught sports
Dick Mainwaring	,, ,, ,,	Elva sports

What is the reason for this sudden increase in the number of fatal racing accidents? It is not speed alone which is dangerous, and it is not in the pure-bred racing car that drivers lose their lives. Nor can the genuine sports car as sold to the public be considered especially unsafe. Admittedly the entries for Sports Car races are far more numerous than for Grands Prix, but there is nothing new in that. Nor was 1955 the first year in which cars of differing speeds and capacities raced on the same circuit.

The new element in motor racing is this—that the regulations of Sports Car events now allow manufacturers to enter sports/racing prototypes which may give a clue to the car of the future but which bear only a superficial resemblance to the article offered to the public. In virtually all cases it is in such machines that drivers have been killed.

One thing is certain; motor racing will not die out for lack of drivers, whatever the risks. There will always be young men who believe that "one crowded hour of glorious life is worth an age without a name", and perhaps it is they who help to keep alive in all of us the spark of resolution.

It may be argued that these contests between prototypes are necessary for the evolution of the motor car; it may be that for every driver killed while racing a hundred week-end motorists will go unharmed. If that is so then the list given above should be headed Roll of Honour.

SLIPSTREAM

THE WRITER of a book such as this is dependent on the goodwill of those whose life and work he is attempting to describe. I would like to acknowledge the invaluable guidance and encouragement I have received from John Eason Gibson of *Country Life* and *Autocourse*.

I owe thanks for their generous help to Count Aymo Maggi of the Brescia Automobile Club, Major Harry Stanley of the R.A.C., Teddy Lawry of the B.A.R.C., and all the race organisers who afforded me facilities. I am indebted to Denis Jenkinson and his editor for the description from *Motor Sport* of Moss's Mille Miglia and to the editor of *Autocourse* for the article by Paul Frere. Of the many expert books on the subject I have most often consulted Laurence Pomeroy's work, *The Grand Prix Car*, and George Monkhouse's *Grand Prix Racing, Facts and Figures*.

Surely a word of praise is due to the Alvis Company who, in 1932, manufactured the car which carried me trouble-free over 10,000 miles of Continental roads to these races of 1955.

Most of all, though, I am indebted to the Racing Drivers themselves.

DOUGLAS RUTHERFORD
Ventimiglia, 1955

TABLE OF PRINCIPAL
RESULTS 1955

EVENTS FOR FORMULA ONE CARS

Argentine Grand Prix. January 16
1. Fangio   Mercedes   77·5 m.p.h.
2. Gonzalez/Trintignant/Farina   Ferrari
3. Farina/Maglioli/Trintignant   Ferrari

Buenos Aires Grand Prix. January 30
1. Fangio   Mercedes   73·43 m.p.h.
2. Moss   Mercedes
3. Trintignant   Ferrari

Turin Grand Prix. March 27
1. Ascari   Lancia   88·4 m.p.h.
2. Mieres   Maserati
3. Villoresi   Lancia

Pau Grand Prix. April 11
1. Behra   Maserati   62·3 m.p.h.
2. Castellotti   Lancia
3. Mieres   Maserati
       Fastest lap: Ascari.   Lancia: 65·4 m.p.h.

Bordeaux Grand Prix. April 24
1. Behra   Maserati   64·65 m.p.h.
2. Musso   Maserati
3. Mieres   Maserati
       Fastest lap: Moss.   Maserati: 67·67 m.p.h.

Daily Express Trophy (Silverstone). May 7
1. Collins   Maserati   95·94 m.p.h.
2. Salvadori   Maserati
3. Bira   Maserati

FORMULA ONE CARS

Naples Grand Prix. **May 8**
1. Ascari   Lancia   68·92 m.p.h.
2. Musso   Maserati
3. Villoresi   Lancia
    Fastest lap: Behra.   Maserati: 70·83 m.p.h.

Monaco Grand Prix. **May 22**
1. Trintignant   Ferrari   65·8 m.p.h.
2. Castellotti
3. Perdisa
    Fastest lap: Fangio.   Mercedes: 68·66

Belgian Grand Prix. **June 5**
1. Fangio   Mercedes   118·76 m.p.h.
2. Moss   Mercedes
3. Farina   Ferrari

Dutch Grand Prix. **June 19**
1. Fangio   Mercedes   89·65 m.p.h.
2. Moss   Mercedes
3. Musso   Maserati
    Fastest lap: Mieres.   Maserati: 92·89 m.p.h.

British Grand Prix. **July 16**
1. Moss   Mercedes   86·47 m.p.h.
2. Fangio   Mercedes
3. Kling   Mercedes

B.A.R.C., International Trophy (Crystal Palace). **July 30**
1. Hawthorn   Maserati   75·75 m.p.h.
2. Schell   Vanwall
3. Salvadori   Maserati
    Fastest lap: Hawthorn ⎫
                 Salvadori ⎬77·94 m.p.h.

Italian Grand Prix. **September 11**
1. Fangio   Mercedes   128·5 m.p.h.
2. Taruffi   Mercedes
3. Castellotti   Ferrari
    Fastest lap: Moss.   Mercedes: 134·8 m.p.h.

SPORTS CARS

Oulton Park Gold Cup.   September 24
1. Moss   Maserati   85·94 m.p.h.
2. Hawthorn   Lancia
3. Titterington   Vanwall

Syracuse Grand Prix.   October 23
1. Brooks   Connaught   99·34 m.p.h.
2. Musso   Maserati
3. Villoresi   Maserati
           Fastest lap: Brooks.   Connaught: 102·357 m.p.h.

SPECIAL CATEGORY

Indianapolis.   500 miles.   May 30.   (*United States*)
1. Sweikert   John Zink Special   128·209 m.p.h.
2. Bettenhausen   Chapman Special
3. Davies   Bardahl Special
         Fastest lap: Vukovich.   Hopkins Special.   141·354 m.p.h.

EVENTS FOR SPORTS CARS

Buenos Aires 1,000 *kilometres.   January* 23
1. Valiente-Ibanez   Ferrari   98·6 m.p.h.
2. Najureto-Rivero   Ferrari
3. Grandio-Faraoni   Maserati

Sebring 12 *hours.   March* 13
1. Hawthorn-Walters   Jaguar   79.3 m.p.h.
2. Hill-Shelby   Ferrari
3. Spear-Johnson   Maserati

British Empire Trophy (*Oulton Park*).   *April* 3
1. Scott-Brown   Lister/Bristol   73.5 m.p.h.
2. McAlpine   Connaught
3. Parnell[1]   Aston-Martin

221

Mille Miglia.   *April* 30—*May* 1
1. Moss   Mercedes   97·9 m.p.h.
2. Fangio   Mercedes
3. Maglioli   Ferrari

Eifelrennen (Germany).   *May* 29
1. Fangio   Mercedes   80·88 m.p.h.
2. Moss   Mercedes   80·88 m.p.h.
3. Gregory   Ferrari
      Fastest lap: Moss.   Mercedes: 83·46 m.p.h.

Supercortemaggiore Grand Prix (Monza).   *May* 29
1. Behra-Musso   Maserati   109·92 m.p.h.
2. Hawthorn-Maglioli   Ferrari
3. Perdisa-Mieres   Maserati

Hyeres 12 *hours.*   *May* 29
1. Canonica-Munaron   Ferrari   83·01 m.p.h.
2. Gaze-MacKay   Aston-Martin
3. Cosh-Cobden   Aston-Martin

Le Mans 24 *hours.*   *June* 11/12
1. Hawthorn-Bueb   Jaguar   107·0 m.p.h.
2. Collins-Frere   Aston-Martin   105·39 m.p.h.
3. Swaters-Claes   Jaguar   103·10 m.p.h.
      Fastest lap: Hawthorn.   Jaguar: 122·31 m.p.h.

Portuguese Grand Prix.   *June* 19
1. Behra   Maserati   92 m.p.h.
2. Gregory   Ferrari
3. Hamilton   Jaguar

Lisbon Grand Prix.   *July* 24
1. Gregory   Ferrari   82·9 m.p.h.
2. De Graffenried   Maserati
3. Godia-Salez   Ferrari

SPORTS CARS

Goodwood 9 *hours* *August* 20
1. Walker-Poore   Aston-Martin   82·24 m.p.h.
2. Titterington-Sanderson   Jaguar
3. Collins-Brooks   Aston-Martin
     Fastest lap: Hawthorn. Jaguar: 91·14 m.p.h.

Swedish Grand Prix (Kristianstad). *August* 7
1. Fangio   Mercedes   100.4 m.p.h.
2. Moss   Mercedes
3. Castellotti   Ferrari

Nurburgring 500 *Kilometres (up to* 1,500 *c.c.*). *August* 28
1. Behra   Maserati   77·5 m.p.h.
2. Von Frankenberg   Porsche
3. Rosenhammer-Barth   E.M.W.

Ulster Tourist Trophy. *September* 17
1. Moss-Fitch   Mercedes   88·32 m.p.h.
2. Fangio-Kling   Mercedes
3. Von Trips-Simon   Mercedes
     Fastest lap: Hawthorn. Jaguar: 94·67 m.p.h.

Targa Florio (Sicily). *October* 16
1. Moss-Collins   Mercedes   59·8 m.p.h.
2. Fangio-Kling   Mercedes
3. Castellotti-Manzon   Ferrari